AF703157

THE A–Z OF COMMERCIAL LEASES

by John Martin, LLB (London), LLM (Michigan),
Solicitor, Director of Property Law Research,
Pinsents

emis
intellectual technology

© John Martin 2003

Published by
emis professional publishing ltd
31–33 Stonehills House
Welwyn Garden City
Hertfordshire
AL8 6PU

ISBN 1 85811 324 5

All rights reserved. No part of this publication may be reproduced, stored in a retrieval system, or transmitted, in any form or by any means, electronic, mechanical, photocopying, recording or otherwise, without the prior permission of the publisher.

The moral right of the author has been asserted.

Typeset by Jane Conway

Cover design by Jane Conway
Cover photography by Jon Adams

Printed in Great Britain by Lightning Source

For Hector Martin

CONTENTS

Chapters

TABLE OF CASES

TABLE OF STATUTES

PREFACE

Four years ago, I was fortunate to have published a short book entitled *Commercial Leases: 50 Traps for the Unwary*. The reviewers for the most part took a kindly attitude and, much to my surprise, the book attracted some buyers. This somewhat longer miscellany is in many ways intended as a companion work. Inevitably there is a partial overlap in terms of subject matter, but the law has moved on in the intervening years. I hope, therefore, that I have managed both to update and to supplement adequately what I wrote on that previous occasion.

My aim, as before, has been to focus on a number of topics that commonly arise in the drafting and negotiating of a commercial lease. In each case, I have concentrated on one or more aspects of the topic in question. In the case of Assignment, for instance, I have concerned myself only with the tests that a landlord might seek to impose in a lease that is a new tenancy. When it comes to Break Rights, on the other hand, I have sought to clean out the cellar!

In particular, I have included commentaries on the Code of Practice for Commercial Leases, the Guide to Good Practice on Service Charges in Commercial Properties, the British Property Federation Short-Term Commercial Lease and the British Property Federation and British Council for Offices Model Clauses for an FRI Office Lease of Whole. I have also reported, in summary, on the presently proposed amendments to the Landlord and Tenant Act 1954. My thoughts on ways of making much greater use of the Heads of Terms stage of a lease negotiation have been thoroughly expounded.

The years that I have spent in practice as a solicitor, and later as a writer and lecturer, have provided a reminder always to me of the time pressures under which all busy property professionals have to work. There can be no substitute for the major text-books in this area, as I said four years ago, but once more I have tried to compress into a comparatively small volume some reminders of basic principles and what I hope are some helpful nuggets of practical advice. They are easy to consume, despite the necessary coating of landlord and tenant law. I should like to think that they will prove attractive not only to property lawyers but also to surveyors and all those who manage commercial properties.

For the avoidance of any doubt, this book is dedicated to my faithful dog.

Finally, I have tried to state the law as at 1st August 2003.

John Martin
Pinsents
1 Park Row
LEEDS
LS1 5AB

1 August 2003

BIOGRAPHICAL DETAILS

JOHN MARTIN, LLB (London), LLM (Michigan), Solicitor

John was admitted as a solicitor in 1972 and ultimately spent 15 years as a partner in a leading City of London firm, specialising in commercial property development and planning law. Now he is Director of Property Law Research with national law firm Pinsents. He speaks frequently at external conferences and has presented well over 700 training seminars to solicitors and surveyors. He also appears in Legal Network Television training videos. For 13 years he has been joint editor of the Estates Gazette's *Planning Notes* feature, and publishes articles in a number of legal periodicals. He is the author of *Commercial Leases – 50 Traps for the Unwary* and a member of the editorial boards of *Landlord & Tenant Review* and *EMIS Property Service*.

ABATEMENT AND SUSPENSION OF RENT

In the absence of any express provision in the lease to the contrary, rent remains payable even though the buildings comprised within the demised premises cannot be used because of damage by fire or other catastrophe. The House of Lords held in *National Carriers Limited* v *Panalpina (Northern) Limited* [1981] AC 675 that the doctrine of frustration would "hardly ever" apply to an executed – as opposed to an executory – lease. Accordingly, frustration will rarely afford a defence to a claim for rent. Despite the catastrophic circumstances, the legal estate remains vested in the tenant. Furthermore, the obligation to pay rent is not one that is regarded as impossible of performance.

No term for abatement or suspension of rent will be implied, even where the tenant has reimbursed the cost of insurance against loss of rent. (See, for instance, *Cleveland Shoe Co Limited* v *Murray's Book Sales (King's Cross) Limited* [1973] 229 EG 1465.) It is vital, therefore, from the tenant's point of view, that a cesser of rent clause appears in the lease, and that it operates whenever the demised premises become unfit for beneficial use in whole or part because they have sustained damage.

These are some issues for landlords to consider:

- Rent cesser should be conditional upon the landlord's policy of insurance not having been vitiated by some act or omission of the tenant or anyone for whom he is responsible.

- In the event of minor damage that is promptly made good, should there be any suspension or abatement at all?

- Will it be more attractive to redevelop than to re-instate (in which case an option to determine in the landlord's favour is required)?

There are also a number of issues for tenants to consider:

- Where an annual rent is payable, for instance, by quarterly instalments in advance, the whole of the quarter's instalment is due on the relevant quarter day. Standard lease wording may not shelter the tenant in respect of the balance of a quarterly instalment where the damage or destruction occurs, for example, a few days into the quarter. Provision needs to be made for repayment of an appropriate proportion of the instalment to the tenant.

- Again, standard lease wording may not protect the tenant where the damage or destruction occurs at the start of the term of the lease, during a rent-free period that has been awarded in the lease itself by means of reservation of a peppercorn or other nominal rent.

- Where the demised premises form part of a larger development, they may themselves go undamaged but damage to the common parts, especially the means of access, may still render them unusable.

- Once the demised premises have been re-instated, will the rent abatement or suspension period extend sufficiently to cover the time it will take for the tenant to fit out the demised premises once more?

- Will the tenant have any ability to determine the lease by notice to the landlord and, if so, in what circumstances? In the case of a short-term lease, this is only reasonable; likewise, where the tenant is concerned about the length of a fixed term abatement or suspension period.

Bear in mind that there will always be instances when it will be appropriate for service charges and insurance premiums to be suspended – or at least abated – as well. It is vital to spell out with clarity exactly which payments are to be suspended in the event of damage or destruction by insured risk. This will always need to be a matter for negotiation.

Factors to be taken into account will include (a) the likelihood that the landlord will still have to maintain some level of insurance cover during the re-instatement period and provide some degree of services, particularly in a multi-let development and (b) the extent of loss of rent cover available under the landlord's insurance policy.

In *P & O Property Holdings Limited* v *International Computers Limited* [1999] 18 EG 158 the issue between the parties was whether the words "the rent" in the cesser of rent clause meant the rack rent reserved by the lease and nothing more, or whether they extended also to the additional rents payable by the tenant in respect of insurance premiums and service charges. Neuberger J decided the former but "not without some difficulty". Clear drafting is essential.

AIRSPACE

There is apparently no clear authority in English law for the proposition that a grant of land carries with it the whole of the space "up to the sky and down to the centre of the earth" following the old maxim *cuius est solum eius est usque ad coelum et ad inferos*. However, it was held in *Bernstein* v *Skyviews and General Limited* [1978] QB 479 that ownership in land, including ownership of a leasehold interest, carries with it by implication the right to the airspace above the land to such height as is necessary for the ordinary use and enjoyment of the land and the structures upon it.

While the decision made it clear that this did not allow a landowner to prevent aircraft flying over his land, other cases have established the right of a tenant to prevent, for instance, the bridging of two buildings by erecting a fire escape over the intervening demised premises, and the oversailing of demised premises by crane-jibs. (See respectively *Straudley Investments Limited* v *Barpress Limited* [1987] 1 EGLR 69 and *Anchor Brewhouse Developments Limited* v *Berkley House (Docklands Developments) Limited* [1987] 2 EGLR 173.) Proceedings for trespass can be taken, but more crucially injunctive relief can be sought.

This militates very much in favour of a landlord restricting the spatial extent of the demise by expressly excluding from it, in the case of a lease of a whole building or the upper portion of a building, the airspace above. The alternative is to define strictly the upper limit of the demised premises by reference to the existing buildings.

First, that will provide an additional means of control over the tenant in relation to upwards expansion. (Covenants against alterations have been known to contain *lacunae* and the relevant covenant may in any event be a qualified one. In addition Part I of the Landlord and Tenant Act 1927 may give the tenant statutory rights to "improve" the premises which cannot be excluded.) The landlord will then be in a position to demand a premium or an increased rent should the tenant propose raising the height of the building, since this would involve a trespass into the landlord's airspace.

Secondly, where the lease has also reserved the appropriate rights in the landlord's favour, it will preserve for the landlord himself the possibility of roof level development. (In this respect, perhaps the most important – albeit frequently overlooked – right is the right of support from the demised premises below. There is no natural right of support for buildings in such circumstances, although such a right may be acquired as an easement.)

Where a landlord has effectively excluded airspace in this way, a properly advised tenant will seek an easement in the lease to enter that airspace to the extent that it is necessary to do so for the purpose of the enjoyment of the demised premises, or compliance with the tenant's obligations in the lease. A tenant may also object where the demised premises include land which has not been built upon. A compromise there might involve excluding airspace over the demised premises above the height of the buildings existing at the date of grant of the lease.

ALTERATIONS

A landlord has a legitimate concern in protecting the nature of his investment and its structure and stability. Nevertheless, an over-restrictive covenant against alterations, particularly one that prevents any development value being realised, can have the effect of depressing rental levels on rent review. It is also important to consider exactly how specific alterations for which consent has been sought and granted should fall to be regarded on rent review, and to make provision accordingly. In addition, commonly overlooked is the issue of whether pre-term alterations, for instance under an agreement for lease, should be taken into account or disregarded at rent review.

Commonly, commercial leases contain absolute covenants against structural alterations and qualified covenants against alterations that do not affect structural components of the subject building. The courts have in the past construed the term "alteration" to mean an alteration in the fabric of the premises or its form and structure, and not necessarily something that changes the appearance of the premises. Ideally, therefore, covenants relating to alterations should deal separately – where appropriate – with matters such as external appearance, layout and merger of two buildings.

Similar problems can arise with the limited construction placed on the word "structure". Frequently it will be necessary to include a definition of what elements in the building are to be regarded as structural elements.

Where the covenant is in qualified form, there is implied into it, by virtue of section 19(2) of the Landlord and Tenant Act 1927, a term that consent may not be unreasonably withheld for the carrying out of improvements. For this purpose, "improvements" have been held to be alterations that improve the premises from the tenant's point of view. (See *F W Woolworth & Co Limited* v *Lambert (No 2)* [1938] Ch 883.) It does not matter that they diminish the value of the premises from the point of view of the landlord. This means, in practice, that in virtually every case a qualified covenant against alterations will be turned into a fully qualified covenant where the alterations or additions in question amount to improvements in that sense. (To put matters beyond doubt, most tenants would argue at lease negotiation for a fully qualified covenant in express terms covering all alterations and additions.)

Section 19(2) goes on to state, *inter alia,* that nothing contained in the sub-section precludes a landlord from requiring, as a condition of consent, an undertaking from the tenant for re-instatement where the improvement does not add to the letting value and where such requirement would be reasonable. This can obviously be dealt with in each individual licence for alterations, but it is probably preferable to deal with re-instatement expressly in the lease by means of a separate absolute covenant. This may well prevent an argument, at the time the terms of the licence are being negotiated, as to whether the requirement is reasonable.

It is usual to bolster a covenant for re-instatement with a provision to the effect that in the event of the tenant failing to re-instate, the landlord is entitled to enter and carry out the necessary works and thereafter charge the cost to the tenant. Caution, perhaps, needs to be exercised in some cases as an automatic entitlement to insist on re-instatement in relation to certain kinds of work to some types of properties might be regarded as depressing rental values at rent review.

Care must be taken when formally requiring re-instatement. In *Westminster City Council* v *HSBC Bank plc* [2003] 1 EGLR 62 the Bank was the tenant of premises on the expiry of a lease for a term of 80 years granted by the Council. The building in question had been designed by Lutyens, on behalf of the Bank, and it contained a number of striking architectural features. The lease imposed restrictions on alterations. Various licences to alter had been granted, obliging the Bank to re-instate when called upon to do so. The Council served a terminal schedule of dilapidations on the Bank, and subsequently issued proceedings claiming damages for breach of covenants in the lease and in the licences. One of two preliminary issues to be tried in the High Court was whether the schedule of dilapidations constituted a notice to re-instate under the various licences. The schedule did not, for instance, refer expressly to the licences though it did refer to "re-instatement".

The deputy judge held that the schedule did amount to sufficient notice, applying the principle established by *Mannai Investment Co Limited* v *Eagle Star Life Assurance Co Limited* [1997] AC 749. A reasonable recipient in the Bank's position would not have been misled as to the Council's intentions. The schedule would be understood to be referring to re-instatement under the licences, since it was only under the licences that re-instatement could be called for.

By way of amendment to a covenant relating to alterations, a tenant's solicitor may well seek a proviso to the effect that – for convenience – consent is not to be required for minor works, such as the installation and removal of demountable partitioning. If the landlord agrees to this he should nevertheless ensure again that the lease provides for re-instatement.

If the point is not covered by a disregard in the rent review provisions, a landlord should also consider imposing an absolute restriction on alterations which reduce the net lettable floor area of the demised premises.

Part I of the Landlord and Tenant Act 1927 provides a means whereby a tenant can override both absolute and qualified covenants against alterations by applying to the court for authorisation to carry out improvements. This involves compliance with a strict procedure and the landlord has an opportunity to be heard if he objects. If the tenant carries out the works pursuant to this procedure, he will generally be entitled to compensation for the improvements on quitting the holding.

Bear in mind, however, that to qualify the improvements must:

- Add to the letting value of the holding at the end of the tenancy.
- Not be trade or other fixtures that the tenant is legally Entitled to remove.
- Be reasonable and suitable to the character of the holding.
- Not diminish the value of any other property belonging to the landlord or any superior landlord.
- Not be made in pursuance of an obligation in a contract made for valuable consideration.

Other statutes, particularly the Disability Discrimination Act 1995, contain provisions that impact on the effect of covenants in leases governing alterations and additions. These must be taken into account at all times.

ASSIGNMENT

The parties to a lease that is a new tenancy for the purposes of the Landlord and Tenant (Covenants) Act 1995 are enabled to prescribe in advance, either in the lease or separately, the circumstances in which the landlord will be entitled to withhold consent to a assignment (but not an underletting) and/or the conditions to which any consent to an assignment may be made subject. This is the effect of provisions inserted by that Act into section 19 of the Landlord and Tenant Act 1927. They apply also to a covenant against parting with possession on assignment.

If consent is subsequently refused on the ground that such circumstances exist, and they do exist, or is given subject to a prescribed condition, the landlord will not be regarded as unreasonably withholding consent, or as giving it subject to unreasonable conditions.

To that extent only, section 19 of the 1927 Act is amended by the 1995 Act. If a landlord seeks to go beyond what has been prescribed in the lease, then the situation will revert to the scrutiny of the court under section 19(1)(a) of the 1927 Act. (This will also be the case where the parties choose not to take advantage of these changes.) By virtue of section 19(1)(a), where there is a covenant, condition or agreement against assigning, underletting, charging or parting with possession of the whole or part of the demised premises without consent, this is deemed to be subject to a proviso that consent cannot be unreasonably held.

Section 1 of the Landlord and Tenant Act 1988 is expressed by the 1995 Act to have effect subject to these new provisions. This section applies where the lease contains a fully qualified prohibition against assigning, underletting, charging or parting with possession of the whole or part of the demised premises. Any person whose consent is required is under a statutory duty to respond to the tenant's application for consent within a reasonable time notifying him in writing whether or not consent is given, if consent is given subject to conditions, what those conditions are and if consent is withheld, the reasons why. Such person is also under a duty to give consent within a reasonable time, unless it is reasonable not to do so.

Section 4 of the 1988 Act provides that a claim may be brought in tort for breach of any of these statutory duties. In *Mount Eden Land Limited* v *Folia* [2003] NPC 95 the judge took the view that exemplary or punitive damages might be available. In the earlier case of *Footwear Corporation Limited* v *Amplight Properties Limited* [1998] 2 EGLR 38 it was held that a landlord could not rely at trial on reasons for refusal that he had failed to communicate in writing to the tenant in compliance with his statutory duty, however reasonable they might be.

The agreement between the parties under the 1995 Act provisions cannot apply to the consent of any third party, e.g. a superior landlord or a mortgagee, and the provisions are not applicable in the case of what might be broadly described as residential leases, or in the case of agricultural holdings or farm business tenancies. The prescribed circumstances and conditions may either be factual or include an element of discretion to be exercised by or on behalf of the landlord. In the latter case the circumstance or condition must *either* state that the discretion is to be exercised reasonably *or* provide that the tenant is to have an unrestricted right to have the determination reviewed conclusively by an independent third party. (The second of these alternatives seems to be the less popular one in drafting practice.)

How should a landlord, in drafting a commercial lease, frame his requirements in relation to applications for a licence to assign? Possibly the only available guidance that comes close to ranking as an industry standard is the Association of British Insurers' Working Party Report of January 1996.

In general the Report:

- Rejected detailed financial tests as being too rigid and unreliable.
- Came down on the side of simplicity by recommending a test of "sufficient financial standing".
- Declined to advocate credit-rating tests because of their backward looking nature.
- Avoided tests involving good estate management grounds.
- Opted for judicial determination of what is 'reasonable' rather than third party determination.
- Recommended an automatic requirement for an authorised guarantee agreement (AGA).
- Offered a clause giving a landlord the ability to refuse consent to an intra-group assignment.
- Offered also a test based on diminution of reversionary value.

It is fair to say that there has been major tenant opposition (and in particular from the British Retail Consortium) to:

- The absolute ban on assignments to associated companies.
- Diminution in value of investment tests.

- The automatic requirement for an AGA.

On this final point, it should be borne in mind that the courts have shown reluctance, in determining the terms of a renewal lease under the Landlord and Tenant Act 1954, to order the insertion of an automatic requirement for an AGA. See *Wallis Fashion Group Limited* v *CGU Life Assurance Limited* [2001] 81 P&CR 28

AUTHORISED GUARANTEE AGREEMENTS

Save in the case of an excluded assignment, a tenant is released on assigning a new tenancy, from future liability under the tenant covenants of the tenancy. (An "excluded assignment" for this purpose is one effected in breach of covenant or occurring by operation of law.) His landlord may, subject to the circumstances set out in section 16(3) of the Landlord and Tenant (Covenants) Act 1995 being met, require him to guarantee performance of the tenant covenants of the tenancy by his assignee. But this can only be done by means of an authorised guarantee agreement (AGA).

As with the form of a contractual guarantor's covenants in a lease, the need for certainty dictates that the required form of AGA should ideally be annexed, or set out as a schedule, to the lease. (Additionally, if it has to be settled at the time consent for an assignment is applied for, it simply adds to the burdens at that time.) But it should not be forgotten that an AGA is a creature of statute and, as such, its content is strictly controlled.

The restrictions contained in section 16(4) of the 1995 Act mean that the AGA may not impose on the outgoing tenant any requirement to guarantee performance of the tenant's covenants other than by the assignee, or any liability in relation to any time after the assignee is released from such covenants by virtue of the Act.

Section 16(5) of the 1995 Act states that an AGA may nevertheless:

- Impose on the outgoing tenant liability as sole or principal debtor.
- Impose on the outgoing tenant liabilities as guarantor which are not more onerous than that liability.
- Require the outgoing tenant, in the event of disclaimer, to enter into a new tenancy for not more than the unexpired residue of the assigned tenancy and containing no more onerous terms.
- Make incidental or supplementary provision.

(Commentators suggest that the courts may well construe "incidental or supplementary provision" in a restrictive manner, but that should not prevent the terms of the AGA dealing with matters such as legal costs, interest on arrears and service of notices etc.)

Within these statutory limitations, the parties are therefore at liberty to specify the terms of the AGA. In practice, its terms will often reflect the provisions of a guarantor's contractual covenants in a modern commercial lease. For the avoidance of any doubt, liability under the AGA should be expressed to subsist notwithstanding that the contractual term of the lease has expired and a continuation tenancy has arisen under section 24 of the Landlord and Tenant Act 1954. The outgoing tenant should also expressly guarantee payment of any interim rent agreed or ordered under section 24A of that Act.

However, if a strict construction is applied to section 16(5), it would not be appropriate for a landlord to seek to impose a requirement on the outgoing tenant to enter into a new lease in the event of premature determination of the original lease, once it is in the hands of the assignee, otherwise than as a result of disclaimer. Equally, he should not seek to provide for payment of additional rent by the outgoing tenant following premature determination of the lease, once in the hands of the assignee, in order to offset letting costs or voids.

It is also doubtful whether a provision requiring the appointment of a replacement for an outgoing tenant who is subject to an AGA and who has met with death, bankruptcy or liquidation, would be effective. (The 1995 Act makes it clear that only an assigning tenant may enter into an AGA.) Again, an outgoing tenant under an AGA cannot be required to join as guarantor in any renewal of the lease as this would involve a different tenancy.

Finally, there must be doubt as to whether the landlord can validly require an indemnity from the tenant under an AGA. (It would appear not to be expressly sanctioned.) Against that, the tenant can be required to accept liability as sole or principal debtor and advantage should be taken of this to cover the possibility in any given case of the assignee failing.

How much of a risk is there in all of this for landlords when drafting an AGA? Perhaps not that much given the wording of sections 16(4) and 25 of the 1995 Act, but a landlord should certainly seek to include wording intended to result in severance of any offending terms.

A tenant will argue that it is only reasonable for a landlord to covenant in an AGA to notify the outgoing tenant promptly in writing of the conclusion of any further assignment of the lease that has the effect of releasing the outgoing tenant from liability under the AGA. The risk otherwise is that this will not come to the knowledge of that outgoing tenant.

BREAK RIGHTS

"Break right" is the term commonly used to describe an option granted to one or both parties to a fixed term lease to terminate the term of that lease before its contractual expiry date. The clause creating the option will need to identify who is entitled to exercise it, the time at which it is capable of being exercised, and the formalities involved.

(Break rights that the parties rarely anticipate exercising appear in most leases. A good example is the right to terminate the lease, following damage or destruction by insured risk, where re-building is frustrated. We are not concerned with those, but rather with break rights negotiated by tenants of business premises having some commercial expediency in mind.)

More difficulties arise in the case of a tenant's rather than a landlord's break right, though a landlord must always bear in mind the interrelationship between the provisions of the Landlord and Tenant Act 1954 and a break right in his favour. Exercise of a landlord's break right merely determines the contractual tenancy, and accelerates commencement of the continuation tenancy under section 24 of that Act, where the Act applies. Little will be gained unless the landlord is in a position simultaneously to serve a section 25 notice opposing renewal. In practice, this frequently means relying on the redevelopment or own occupation grounds. A landlord should therefore ideally seek to insist upon the lease being contracted out of the Act.

A tenant merely has to serve the contractual break notice. Once that has been served, it is no longer open to the tenant to serve a request for a new tenancy. (See section 26(4) of the Act.) But there are a number of pitfalls for tenants to avoid in negotiating a break right. Failure to avoid them will frequently result in an insoluble problem for the tenant, at the time when the break right becomes exercisable. In many cases, the break right will be lost.

These are some of the issues that may well arise in that context.

Is the break right to be personal to the Tenant?

A landlord will frequently try the damage limitation exercise – as far as investment value is concerned – of seeking to insist that the break right is personal to the original tenant, and is not to be exercisable by successors in title. If circumstances then bring about an early assignment or transfer of the lease, the landlord is the winner.

The problem for the tenant here is corporate re-organisations. On a letting to a company within a group of companies, this point does need to be borne in mind and specific provision made. In *Brown & Root Technology Limited* v *Sun Alliance and London Assurance Limited* [1997] 1 EGLR 39, for instance, this had not been done, with the result that the break right appeared to have been lost on an intra-group transfer of the lease. Only the fact that the transfer had not been registered at H M Land Registry, so leaving the legal estate in the lease vested in the original tenant, preserved the break right.

What happens in such circumstances if the lease is subsequently assigned or transferred back to the original tenant? Much depends upon the wording of the break right in question, but the decision in *Equinox Industrial Limited* v *Sketchley Limited* [2003] NPC 13 is one of a line of decisions holding that the break right does not survive. (Such a result must in any event be inevitable if the landlord has insisted on the break right being expressed not only as personal to the original tenant but also to lapse automatically on the first assignment or transfer of the lease. This is not uncommon.)

Should the Tenant be entitled unilaterally to waive the break right?

A break right for which the commercial need subsequently disappears – because, for instance, the tenant's business proves successful – can cause embarrassment for the tenant at rent review, where it carries over into the hypothetical lease. (See below.) This can be avoided if the tenant is entitled to waive the break right by notice served on the landlord at any time.

Will vacant possession be required on the break date?

The answer will almost invariably be in the affirmative. There is nothing to be negotiated here with the landlord. The tenant must simply be aware of this requirement in the context of any underlease that he may subsequently negotiate.

The Court of Appeal held in *Pennell* v *Payne* [1995] 1 EGLR 6 that the exercise of a tenant's break right operates also to determine any underlease. But the story does not end there. Any such underlease should be granted outside the Landlord and Tenant Act 1954. Otherwise, the undertenant may well be in a position to prevent the tenant from giving vacant possession. In addition, its term should expire prior to the break date, or there should be a corresponding break right, if the tenant is to avoid being exposed to an action by the undertenant on the covenant for quiet enjoyment in the underlease.

When should the break date ideally fall?

In a nutshell, from the tenant's point of view, on the day immediately preceding a rent payment day. This is because rent payable in advance is not apportionable once it accrues and becomes due. There is apparently no direct authority on this point in the context of break rights. However, it was held in *William Hill (Football) Limited* v *Willen Key & Hardware Limited* [1964] 190 EG 867 that where a tenant surrendered a lease between rent payment dates, the tenant was not entitled to any refund in respect of rent paid in advance, in the absence of some agreement to the contrary.

Other factors also govern the choice of the actual break date. The tenant should therefore ensure, at the negotiating stage, that an express provision requiring repayment by the landlord of the proper apportioned amount of all rents paid in advance is included.

Will payment of a liquidated sum be required from the Tenant?

Here a point of general concern for tenants arises. A break right is in the nature of an option. This must never be ignored. Accordingly, its terms will be strictly construed, and strict compliance with those terms will generally be required if the break right is to be validly exercised and the lease brought to an end. Time will be of the essence, in the absence of a provision to the contrary.

Landlords frequently seek to negotiate provision for payment of a liquidated sum – often measured by reference to the current passing rent – on the exercise of the tenant's break right. (If nothing more, this can help soften the effect of any resulting void.) Usually, the requirement will be for payment to be made on or before the break date. In the absence of wording to the contrary, such an obligation will be viewed as a strict pre-condition to termination of the lease.

In *Credit Lyonnais SA* v *Russell Jones & Walker* [2002] 2 EGLR 65 exercise of the tenant's break right required the giving of six months' prior notice and payment of the sum of £11,500 "not later than the Termination Date". The requisite notice was served but the sum remained unpaid on the Termination Date. The landlord successfully argued that the break right had not been validly exercised. The tenant had to buy its way out of the lease. The tenant's solicitors were held to have been negligent in failing to warn the tenant that time was of the essence in relation to payment of the sum.

In the earlier case of *Dun & Bradstreet Software Services (England) Limited* v *Provident Mutual Life Association* [1998] 2 EGLR 175 it was also held that time was of the essence in respect of payment of a penalty rent. Failure to pay on time meant that the break right had not been validly exercised.

All that the tenant can do at the heads of terms stage is to negotiate for an express provision to the effect that time is not of the essence in relation to the payment of any liquidated sum, or at least for some period of grace.

Is the exercise of the break right in any way linked to rent review?

There are at least two specific problems for the tenant here.

If the break right has been negotiated so as to provide the tenant with an escape route in the event that he is unhappy with the outcome of the rent review, there will be an obvious interrelationship between the break clause and the rent review clause. This may result in any time limits within the rent review clause being regarded, by implication, as strict ones. (In other words, the presumption that time is not of the essence will be rebutted.) An example of this can be found in *Al-Saloom* v *Shirley James Travel Services Limited* [1981] 259 EG 420.

Clearly, this is not in the interest of either party. Ideally, the break provisions should form an integral part of the rent review clause, time should be expressed not to be of the essence and the break right should become exercisable by notice only upon conclusion of the rent review.

The second problem is an associated one. The landlord must not be allowed to deprive the tenant of its break right by seeking to frustrate the rent review process. This could happen where the landlord is solely entitled to initiate the review.

In *Johnsons of London Limited* v *Protec Trust Management* [2000] EGCS 114 the tenant was entitled to break "at any time before a date being fifty-six days after the final determination of the rent review". The landlord had the sole right to initiate the rent review, which was an either way one. The first review was due in March 1999. He chose not to implement the review because rent levels had fallen over the relevant period. The tenant, nevertheless, purported to exercise the break right in April 1999, and sought a declaration in the High Court that the lease had been validly determined. The judge refused the declaration, accepting the landlord's argument that the right to break could not be divorced from the making of an actual rent determination.

It is essential that the rent review provisions in such a case give the tenant an equal opportunity to initiate the rent review, and an ability to prosecute it to a prompt conclusion.

What about the state of repair at the break date?

A landlord will always expect the premises to be handed back in a state of repair consistent with proper performance of the tenant's repairing and decorating obligations in the lease. It is at least some recompense for premature termination of the lease, and it assists in prompt marketing of the vacant premises. If this is made a strict pre-condition, the likelihood is that the tenant will try hard to comply and a dilapidations claim will not be necessary. But what if the tenant in some way falls short of the required level of performance? Uncertainty results and the break right may well be lost. It could be said that the landlord has given with one hand – in granting the break right – and taken away with the other – by imposing a strict pre-condition relating to repair.

There is a way of giving both parties what they want. The tenant's obligation should be to deliver the premises up at the break date in the required state and condition or pay compensation in lieu. (That will require the insertion of a short provision for third party determination of the amount of the compensation if the parties cannot agree.) Provided that the tenant does one or the other, the break right remains exercisable.

Will the Tenant be required to comply with any other lease obligations?

Invariably again, the answer to this will be in the affirmative. As a minimum, the landlord will require payment by the break date of all rent accrued due at that point and vacant possession.

It may also be a pre-condition that the tenant has complied with other covenants contained in the lease. (See below.) For the moment, let us simply consider what should be the relevant date for compliance. Ideally, from the tenant's point of view, this should be the break date itself. If it is an earlier date – such as the date for service of the break notice – there will always be the risk that this is overlooked, or that the tenant will have allowed himself insufficient time to comply.

The worst position for the tenant to be in is one where the tenant's history of compliance with his obligations is to be brought into account. This may come about, for instance, where the condition refers to the tenant "having complied with his obligations under this Lease". Such a situation should be avoided. The landlord's only concern should be with state of affairs at the break date.

If so, what degree of compliance should be required?

Where possible, the tenant should try to avoid the exercise of the break right being conditional upon anything other than payment of all rent accrued due at the break date and vacant possession. If possible "rent" should be limited to rack rent properly demanded.

If the landlord is in a position to insist upon some degree of compliance with other covenants at the break date, then this should be restricted to "reasonable" compliance, or an absence of "material" breaches. (Without such wording, strict compliance will be required and even some trivial breach of covenant – unless it is a spent breach – will prevent the valid exercise of the break right.)

Even where words of limitation do appear, uncertainty is likely to flow. This can be seen from the decision in *Commercial Union Life Assurance Co Limited* v *Label Ink Limited* [2001] L & TR 29. Here, the tenant's break right was conditional upon (a) payment of rent due, and (b) an absence of material breaches of covenant by the break date.

The final instalment of rent for part of the relevant quarter was paid by means of a cheque posted after the rent payment date and before the break date. The landlord received the cheque after the break date. No doubt to the tenant's relief, the judge held, on the basis of decided cases, that the rent had still been paid by the break date.

The judge also held that, while the cumulative effect of various breaches of the tenant's repairing covenant might be regarded as material, they should not be so regarded because (i) the cost of remedial works was only £12,000, (ii) the tenant had genuinely sought to comply and had followed professional advice, and (iii) the landlord had been not so much concerned with compliance as with taking advantage of non-compliance. (In other words, he considered that a range of factors had to be taken into account in determining materiality.)

However, he held that late payment of the final instalment of rent – albeit technically paid by the break date – did amount to a material breach of covenant in the circumstances of this case. (The landlord could not be certain at the break date whether the lease had been determined.) This material breach deprived the tenant of its right to break.

What impact should the break right have at rent review?

The existence of a break right in a lease will inevitably influence rental value.

Perhaps the first point to note is that if the break right is expressed to be personal to the tenant, it will not carry over into the hypothetical lease in the absence of express wording. So decided the Court of Appeal in *St Martin's Property Investments Limited* v *CIB Properties Limited* [1999] L & TR 1. (This accords generally with the principle that anything in the nature of a concession personal to the actual tenant would not be available to the hypothetical tenant.)

This approach will not necessarily be acceptable to a landlord and in any case, the lease should always spell out whether the break clause is to form part of the hypothetical lease. As a separate issue, it should also be made clear by express wording the point at which during the hypothetical term, the break right is to be available to the hypothetical tenant.

For instance, in *R & A Millett (Shops) Limited* v *Legal & General Assurance Society Limited* [1985] 1 EGLR 103 the lease contained a break clause operable after the twelfth year of the term on six months' notice. It was held that the rent to be paid on the rent review at the expiry of the twelfth year of the term should be assessed on the footing of a hypothetical lease terminable on six months' notice.

In conclusion, if a tenant has sought to negotiate a break right at the outset, it is likely to be of crucial commercial importance to him. He will need to know that when the time comes for its exercise, he is capable of bringing this about. It is therefore one of those aspects of a commercial lease that deserves particular attention at the heads of terms stage.

CODE OF PRACTICE ON COMMERCIAL LEASES

The present Government has consistently expressed concern that the commercial property industry does not provide the business sector with sufficient breadth of choice when lease terms are offered. In particular, it has criticised the practice of upward only rent reviews. The Labour Party's Business Manifesto of June 2001 stated "Upward only rent reviews are a source of grievance to many in the business community. We will promote greater flexibility in the commercial property market". The Government was undoubtedly fuelled by the disappointing results of research carried out by Reading University into the effectiveness of the earlier (1995) voluntary Code of Practice.

In September 2000 it convened what became known as the Commercial Leases Working Group, a joint working party representing a wide range of interests within the property industry, and a number of governmental and professional bodies. The Group was charged with drafting and agreeing a new version of the Code that would include proposals for more flexible leases and alternatives to upward only rent reviews. This was against the background of repeated threats by the Government of legislation as an alternative to self-regulation.

On 22nd April 2002, the Government officially launched the new version of the Code of Practice on Commercial Leases. It also outlined a three-point package of monitoring, involving feedback from the industry, analysis of complaints and research with what was then an interim report at the end of the first year.

The Government subsequently commissioned Reading University to report on market reaction to the Code and its implementation. An interim report is now expected late in 2003. If that report is unfavourable, there must be a good chance that the Government will begin a consultation process with a view to legislation.

The Code, which also contains guidance notes in plain English, sets out ten recommendations for landlords and tenants on the negotiation of a business lease and a further 13 recommendations governing conduct during a lease. These were considered by the Group to reflect best practice. Probably the most controversial recommendation is the following one:

> *"Rent reviews should generally be to open market rent. Wherever possible, landlords should offer alternatives which are priced on a risk-adjusted basis, including alternatives to upwards only rent reviews; these might include up/down reviews to open market rent with a minimum of the initial rent, or another basis such as annual indexation. Those funding property should make every effort to avoid imposing restrictions on the length of lease and type of rent review that landlords, developers and/or investors may offer."*

In the same vein, the Code says that landlords should consider offering tenants a choice of length of term, including break clauses where appropriate, and with or without security of tenure. Where alternative lease terms are offered, different rents should be appropriately priced for each set of terms.

Attempts are made to deal with various traditional complaints on the part of business occupiers. The tenant's repairing obligations, and any repair costs included in the service charge, should be appropriate to the length of the term. Buildings insurance policy terms should be competitive, and the tenant of an entire building should be given the opportunity to influence the choice of insurer.

Generally, the only restriction on an assignment of the whole should be the requirement to obtain the landlord's consent, and that consent must not be unreasonably withheld. An authorised guarantee agreement should only be required where the assignee is of lower financial standing than the assignor. Landlords are also required to observe the Guide to Good Practice on Service Charges in Commercial Properties. (See below.)

Critics might be forgiven for saying that many of the recommendations are aimed simply at encouraging prospective tenants to exercise business common sense. Those recommendations that are more radical are couched in terms that can hardly be described as mandatory. (It is implicit in the drafting that a number of compromises had to be reached. This should cause no surprise, given the divergent interests within the Group.) It might also be questioned how many leases the Code is likely to influence. It is apparently not to apply in the case of lettings in force at the time of publication. On the grant of most underleases, there will be little scope for its application, and on the renewal of an existing lease, statute presently governs the content if the parties fail to agree. Where it is to apply, the absence of any obvious specific sanction may strip it of all effectiveness unless the commercial property industry collectively recognises the threat of future legislation.

The view of many within the industry is that the new Code is unnecessary. Market forces have produced considerable change over the years since 1995, and the research by Reading University backs this up. Average lease lengths have dropped across all sectors. Many leases are granted for terms of less than five years and so without provision for rent review. Tenant's break rights become increasingly common. Landlords are more inclined today to see themselves as providing a product to a customer. Many such customers would not want to pay premium prices for the alternative terms that the Code refers to.

Against that, the British Property Federation is determined to encourage the commercial property industry to adopt the Code. It has published on its website a number of resources to aid compliance with the Code. (See www.bpf.org.uk/publications/comleases.php.) These include a checklist, model letter clauses, advice on compliance, a monitoring questionnaire, a logo and the means (for BPF members) of registering as promoters of the Code.

For the moment, the practical problems lie with landlords and their surveyors but to the extent that solicitors do become involved in the negotiations of heads of terms on the grant of a lease, the legal profession is not immune.

COMPENSATION

A landlord of business premises needs to be aware, even at the lease negotiation stage, of the circumstances in which he may be called upon to pay compensation at some future date to his tenant. For instance, Parliament's intention in 1954 was that a tenant should be compensated for the loss of his right to renew his business tenancy where the ground relied upon by his landlord is one of three specific grounds of opposition not involving any fault on the tenant's part, namely:

- Uneconomic sub-letting of part by the landlord.
- Demolition or reconstruction by the landlord.
- Occupation by the landlord for the purposes of a business or as a residence.

Under section 37 of the Landlord and Tenant Act 1954, the right of a business tenant to claim compensation, for what is effectively disturbance, presently arises in three situations, namely:

1 Where the only stated grounds of opposition are those set out in paragraphs (e), (f) or (g) of section 30(1) of the Act and no application is made to the court by the tenant. (It is not even necessary for the tenant to serve a counter-notice to the landlord's section 25 notice to retain his entitlement to compensation.)

2 Where the only stated grounds of opposition are those set out in paragraphs (e), (f) or (g) of section 30(1) of the Act the tenant applies to the court but

withdraws his application. (The tenant cannot be required to give up compensation where leave for withdrawal is required.)

3 Where the tenant's application is dismissed by the court on the landlord successfully opposing that application on one or more of the grounds set out in paragraphs (e), (f) or (g). (Where the landlord states an additional ground or grounds, no compensation is payable unless, on the application of the tenant under section 37(4) of the Act, the court certifies that one or more of the grounds set out in paragraphs (e), (f), and (g) has been made out, and that no other ground has been.)

Therefore, the statement of an additional ground in the landlord's section 25 notice, or in his counter-notice to the tenant's section 26 request, forces a tenant into court if he is to preserve his claim for compensation. This is a tactical step open to a landlord where an additional ground is available to him.

It clearly follows that where the tenant's application is dismissed on any ground other than those set out in paragraphs (e), (f) and (g), no compensation will be payable under section 37.

The tenant becomes entitled to compensation on quitting the holding. In *Webb* v *Sandown Sports Club Limited* [2000] EGCS 13 the judge equated "quitting" for this purpose with ceasing business occupation, even though this occurred before the extended termination date of the tenancy.

By virtue of section 37(2) of the Act, compensation is calculated by reference to the rateable value of the holding, subject to separate rules governing the situation where "domestic property" is included within the holding. The amount of compensation is equal to *either* one times the rateable value times the "appropriate multiplier" *or* two times the rateable value times the "appropriate multiplier". The "appropriate multiplier" is prescribed by the Secretary of State by statutory instrument and, ignoring transitional cases, at present its value is one. (See the Landlord and Tenant Act 1954 (Appropriate Multiplier) Order 1990.)

The higher rate of compensation (two times the rateable value times the appropriate multiplier) is only available to the tenant where the conditions laid down in section 37(3) of the Act are satisfied. These are that either:

- The tenant has himself occupied the holding, or part of the holding, for the purposes of a business for the whole of the 14 years immediately preceding the termination date specified in either the section 25 notice or section 26 request, or

- The tenant is a successor to a business which has been carried on at the premises for that period.

It is important to note that the tenant will lose his right to the higher rate of compensation if he moves out earlier. See *Sight & Sound Education Limited* v *Books Etc Limited* [1999] 3 EGLR 45.

It is not clear exactly what is meant by "successor" to a business. Possibly the tenant would need to show that he had acquired the goodwill of the business, or inherited the same clientele. The previous occupier need not have been a tenant himself. He might, for instance, be the landlord of the tenant, having granted a lease to him and transferred the business to him.

The parties to a lease may contract out of the statutory obligation to pay compensation for disturbance. Commonly, landlords seek to insist upon this. But if section 38(2) of the Act applies, any such agreement will be void. That provision applies:

> *"Where (a) during the whole of the five years immediately preceding the date on which the tenant under a tenancy to which this Part of this Act applies is to quit the holding, premises being or comprised in the holding have been occupied for the purposes of a business carried on by the occupier or for those and other purposes and (b) if during those five years there was a change in the occupier of the premises, the person who was the occupier immediately after the change was the successor to the business carried on by the person who was the occupier immediately before the change".*

The safer view is that reference to the date upon which the tenant "is to quit the holding" is a reference to the date upon which he is legally obliged to give up possession. This was implicitly approved by the Court of Appeal in *Bacchiocchi* v *Academic Agency Limited* [1998] 3 EGLR 157. However, in that case the appeal judges held that the requirements of section 38(2) were still satisfied notwithstanding that the tenant had wound down his business and vacated some 13 days earlier than the date on which the tenancy terminated.

As separate matters it should be noted that:

- The court may order the landlord to pay compensation under section 55 of the Act if it subsequently appears that the court refused to order the grant of a new tenancy as a result of the landlord having made a misrepresentation or having concealed material facts. (This will not apply at present where as a result of the misrepresentation the tenant has withdrawn his application to the court, or has simply not applied.)

- As we have seen already, the tenant may qualify for compensation for improvements under Part I of the Landlord and Tenant Act 1927.

DEEMED SURRENDER AND RE-GRANT

A surrender results in the lease merging in the immediate reversion and becoming extinguished. It may either be made expressly – in which case Section 52 of the Law of Property Act 1925 requires a deed – or occur by operation of law. The latter requires some act by the parties that is inconsistent with the continuation of the lease, in circumstances where it would then be unreasonable for them to rely upon the fact that the lease had not been surrendered. A clear example of a surrender by operation of law would be where the tenant gives up possession of the premises and the landlord accepts it. An objective test is applied and intention is irrelevant. The principle is based upon estoppel.

Whether a purported variation of a lease takes effect as a surrender and re-grant by operation of law depends upon the nature of the variation. The Court of Appeal held in *Friends' Provident Life Office* v *British Railways Board* [1995] 2 EGLR 55 that such a consequence would only result where the variation affected the legal estate. This meant either (a) an extension to the existing term of the lease, or (b) the addition of further premises to those already demised.

It is not rare in practice to find a landlord and tenant entering into negotiations part way through the currency of a lease that may well involve an extension of the term or an addition to the demised premises. The consequences of a deemed surrender and re-grant coming about can be serious for the landlord, for the following reasons at least:

- The surrender will release from future liability former tenants and guarantors who remain bound by the covenants in the lease. (In theory, this should include a former tenant who remains liable under an authorised guarantee agreement.)

- Where the lease has been excluded from the operation of sections 24 to 28 of the Landlord and Tenant Act 1954, the effect of the court order and the exclusion agreement will not extend to the fresh lease. (The tenant will acquire security of tenure.)

- By virtue of section 1(5) of the Landlord and Tenant (Covenants) Act 1995, where the deemed surrender and re-grant occurs on or after 1st January 1996 the fresh lease has effect as a new tenancy for the purposes of that Act, regardless of the date of grant of the original lease. (For instance, the tenant will enjoy an automatic release from future liability on an assignment.)

The tenant needs to bear in mind that stamp duty, and possibly Land Registry fees will become payable.

Where the term is to be extended, a reversionary lease should be granted. Where premises are to be added, resort should be had to a supplemental lease. In each case this will preserve the original lease intact, albeit that the further lease will have effect as a new tenancy.

A number of basic drafting points arise.

- Any reversionary lease should be granted upon the express basis that if the original lease suffers premature determination for whatever reason, the reversionary lease becomes absolutely void. Each lease must be incapable of being assigned separately. It may also be necessary to extend the term of the notional lease on rent review.

- In the case of a supplemental lease, thought must be given as to whether permitted assignments and sub-lettings should now be restricted to the extended premises as a whole. Likewise, the rent review provisions must require the interest of the tenant in the whole of the premises to be taken into account on each occasion.

It is far from clear whether a reduction in the length of the term will also result in a deemed surrender and re-grant. The better drafting approach in such a case would be to prepare an agreement for surrender of the lease on the revised termination date, and apply for the appropriate court order under section 38(4) of the 1954 Act.

On a strict reading of the *Friends Provident* case, it seems unlikely that a surrender of part of the demised premises, even if coupled with an abatement of the rent, will amount to a deemed surrender and re-grant.

For further comments on surrenders, see below.

DEMISED PREMISES

Undoubtedly, law students have been told since time immemorial that the most important part of any lease from the point of view of the need for precise drafting is the parcels clause or, to use slightly more modern terminology, the definition of the demised premises. If there is any error or ambiguity, it will repeat itself many times over. That definition will govern the physical extent of the respective rights and duties of the parties to the lease, including, for instance, any rights of renewal that the tenant may have under the Landlord and Tenant Act 1954. It may also impact on the ability of the landlord to oppose renewal under that Act on the ground that he intends to demolish or reconstruct.

Section 62 of the Law of Property Act 1925 implies wide general wording into a conveyance of land so as to include, for instance, buildings, fixtures, fences, cellars, areas, and courtyards to the extent that they appertain or are reputed to appertain to the land. However, this implication can be overridden by the wording of the conveyance itself. As the word "conveyance" is expressly defined in section 205 of the Act to include a lease it is important in the case of modern leases to be conscious of the uncertainties that can flow in the event that such general wording is allowed to govern the extent of rights and duties. A similar problem may flow from a number of general presumptions that are recognised. (See, for instance, the earlier comments on airspace.)

Save possibly where the whole of the land comprised within a registered title is being let, a plan of appropriate scale should always be used. Where there are no satisfactory points of identification on the ground, measurements should be shown on the plan. Where the letting is of part only of a building, it is preferable for detailed drawings to be used. (Inevitably, in this last case, the draftsman will need to inspect the premises.) As from 13th October 2003, leases granted for a term exceeding seven years require to be registered at HM Land Registry and a plan is compulsory where such a lease is granted in respect of part of the land within a registered title. The lease plan will also have relevance where measurement is required on rent review.

It is important that the lease provides whether the plan is to prevail over the written description or vice versa in the event of conflict. Phrases such as "more particularly delineated" should secure that the plan prevails, since they indicate an intention that the plan should define the actual boundaries of the land. Phrases such as "for the purpose of identification only" should prevent the plan from prevailing over the written description since they indicate an intention to define location only.

It is, however, important to take into account in that context Part I of the Law of Property (Miscellaneous Provisions) Act 1994. In *Parker-Lake Homes Limited* v *Morgan* [2003] NPC 44 the seller sold and transferred to the buyer a plot of unregistered land. The plan annexed to the contract and the transfer was detailed and professionally drawn, albeit that it was stated to be "for the purposes of identification only". The sale was expressed to be with full title guarantee. When the buyer sought to register the transfer, it transpired that a strip of the land in question was already registered in the name of a third party. Ultimately, the buyer had to acquire the land from that third party for £20,000. The buyer sued the seller relying upon section 2 of the 1994 Act.

The trial judge held that the seller was in breach of the covenant implied by section 2(1)(a) of the 1994 Act, i.e.

that the person making the disposition has the right to dispose of the property as he purports to so do. He awarded damages including a sum equalling the cost of acquiring the disputed land from the third party. The seller was purporting to transfer to the buyer land right up to the boundaries that were specifically shown on a professionally drawn plan. The use of the phrase "for the purpose of identification only" was insufficient for the purposes of section 8 of the 1994 Act, i.e. the ability of the parties to limit or extend the terms of any of the implied covenants by express wording in the instrument of transfer.

Finally, the description of the premises should take into account expressly fences and other boundary structures. If it does not, there may well be *lacunae* in relation to the covenants for repair and alteration etc. The definition should also be worded so as to include fixtures and fittings and all additions, alterations and improvements made during the term, so that the tenant's covenants, whether contained in the lease or in any subsequent supplemental deed, automatically extend to them.

Section 62 of the Law of Property Act 1925 also provides that a conveyance of land includes, and operates to convey with the land, "all... liberties, privileges, easements, rights and advantages appertaining or reputed to appertain to the land at the time of the conveyance". As we have seen, this will apply also in the case of a lease (although not in the case of a mere agreement for lease). The sub-section will even operate to create new legal rights by converting informal or concessionary arrangements into such rights.

The rule in *Wheeldon* v *Burrows* (1879) 12 Ch D 31 needs to be considered in the same context. Generally speaking, this will operate in a similar way to pass continuous and apparent easements on a conveyance or lease of part and will also apply in the case of a contract for sale or letting.

Both provide a considerable fall-back for a tenant of commercial premises where less than adequate provision has been made in the lease for the express grant of appropriate easements. At the same time, however, each can work to the detriment of a landlord, and best practice dictates that on the grant of a lease of part of the premises in a landlord's ownership, each is excluded.

Section 62(4) of the 1925 Act allows this in that it provides that the section does not apply where a contrary intention is expressed in the conveyance. Likewise, the rule in *Wheeldon* v *Burrows* can be excluded in the contract or conveyance. The tenant must then rely upon the easements expressly granted by the lease, and which will no doubt have been the subject of pre-lease negotiation. The landlord's retained land will then go free from incumbrance by additional and (often) unnecessary easements arising in favour of the tenant which might otherwise further restrict the ability of the landlord to deal with that retained land.

The decision of the Court of Appeal in *Pretoria Warehousing Co Limited* v *Shelton* [1993] EGCS 120 illustrates that clear and unambiguous wording is required to exclude the operation of section 62 and provides an example of the consequences of failing to do so effectively. In that case, the landlord had granted leases of self-contained retail units grouped around a central concourse in a shopping centre. The tenants and their customers had unlimited use of the whole concourse area. Subsequently, the landlord took back an area of the central concourse and formed a new letting unit from it, so depriving customers of the ability to circulate freely.

The tenants sought an injunction. The Court of Appeal held that there had been an interference with the easements to use the whole of the concourse that had passed, by virtue of section 62, on the grant of the leases. Furthermore, the express grant in the leases of an easement in limited terms to use the concourse did not amount to a contrary intention for the purposes of section 62(4). Clear and unambiguous wording was required.

In *Hair* v *Gillman* [2000] 3 EGLR 74, the appellant had taken a lease of a self-contained building in 1972. Seven years later, she purchased the building from her landlord. In the meantime, with her landlord's permission, she had parked cars on his adjoining forecourt. The Court of Appeal held that even though the permission did not amount to an easement or an implied grant between 1972 and 1979, and even though the permission was precarious (in the sense that it could have been withdrawn at any time) nevertheless it crystallised into an easement by virtue of section 62 on the conveyance of the building to her.

For an example of a problem arising in the context of a part disposal of freehold land, see *P & S Platt Limited* v *Crouch* [2003] NPC 97. In that case, the seller owned a freehold riverside hotel on the Norfolk Broads and, separately, a set of moorings and a bungalow situated on an island in the river. There was a footbridge link. The moorings were made available to those hotel guests who arrived by boat. Signs in the grounds of the bungalow made it clear that the moorings were for the exclusive use of hotel guests.

The seller entered into an agreement with the buyer for the sale of the hotel as a going concern. (Neither the sale agreement nor the subsequent transfer of the hotel made any reference to the moorings.) Simultaneously, the seller granted the buyer an option to purchase the bungalow and the moorings but the buyer failed to exercise that option within the prescribed time limit. The seller then denied that there was any entitlement in the buyer to use the moorings. The buyer contended that the right to use them had passed by virtue of section 62.

At first instance it was held that the right to enjoy the moorings had passed to the buyer by virtue of section 62. Furthermore, the right to moor boats to mooring posts and the right to place notices or signs were established categories of easements. The judge also declined to rectify the sale agreement and transfer. The seller appealed to the Court of Appeal on the section 62 issue. The appeal was dismissed. The rights in question clearly appertained to, and were reputed to appertain to and to be enjoyed with, the hotel – being part of the hotel business. Section 62 therefore operated to convert them into full easements. The rule in *Wheeldon* v *Burrows* also applied.

Bear in mind that neither section 62 nor the rule in *Wheeldon* v *Burrows* will assist a landlord when it comes to the question of the reservation of easements. It is essential that these are reserved expressly and in full in the landlord's favour. (It was held in *Re Webb's Lease* [1952]

Ch 808 that a landlord will be entitled to rights that are in their nature reciprocal to easements that he has granted to the tenant, but it is preferable not to rely upon this.)

While in certain circumstances an easement of necessity may be allowed, a landlord should always set out expressly, as exceptions and reservations, the rights which he will require to be retained over the demised premises. It is essential to take specific instructions from a landlord client as to the extent of both present and future rights that will be needed to protect and benefit the retained land.

Commonly, a landlord will need to reserve rights of entry onto the demised premises for the purpose of carrying out works of repair that he is not under an obligation to carry out himself, together with works of repair to adjoining premises (including the common parts) and works of improvement to both. Rights in relation to services and access may be required as well as a right of escape in the case of fire or other emergency.

The possibility of future development of the retained land must always be borne in mind, particularly in relation to rights of light and air that might be enjoyed or subsequently acquired by the demised premises.

A further specific right that is often overlooked in the case of retail units is the right to erect temporary scaffolding. Without such a right the landlord may face a claim for damages for breach of the covenant for quiet enjoyment. See *Owen* v *Gadd* [1956] 2 QB 99. It is also sensible to reserve a right of entry in connection with rent reviews and lease renewals. A reservation that is increasingly incorporated into leases, is the right to enter onto the property with environmental consultants etc. for the purpose of carrying out investigations to ascertain whether the tenant's use of the property has resulted in contamination or pollution.

FIXED CHARGES AND OVERRIDING LEASES

Modern forms of commercial lease invariably also reserve as rent all other money payments due from the tenant under the lease. (The alternative is to leave them as mere contractual payments.) The perceived advantages of this drafting approach are that in the event of default, section 146 of the Law of Property Act 1925 will have no application, and the remedy of distress should be available.

At times, too much emphasis can be placed upon this. Relief from forfeiture for non-payment of rent may still be obtained, and distress will not be appropriate in any circumstances where there is doubt as to the certainty of the sums alleged to be due. (It also seems probable that the law of distress will be radically reformed by statute in due course.)

There may even be disadvantages in this drafting approach since the coming into effect of section 17 of the Landlord and Tenant (Covenants) Act 1995. This provision requires a landlord (irrespective of whether the lease constitutes a new tenancy or an old tenancy for the purposes of that Act) to serve a prescribed form of default notice upon any former tenant or former guarantor whom the landlord seeks to pursue for payment of what the Act refers to as a "fixed charge". The notice must be served within six months of the sum in question falling due for payment. Failure to do so means that the landlord will be unable to recover that sum from the third party in question.

"Fixed charge" is defined so as to include rent – which is assumed to mean any money reserved as rent – service charges, insurance premiums and any liquidated sum payable under the lease for failure to comply with a tenant covenant. It follows that many payments due under a lease will automatically qualify as fixed charges for this purpose, but those which do not will be brought within the statutory definition by virtue of being reserved as rent. In turn, this means that a section 17 notice will be a requisite on many more occasions when the current tenant defaults.

How does this amount to anything more than a minor inconvenience for the landlord? Section 17 must always be read in conjunction with section 19 of the same Act. A former tenant or former guarantor who, having received a section 17 notice, makes full payment of the specified fixed charge is entitled to claim an overriding lease of the premises from the landlord within 12 months. The claimant, on the grant of the overriding lease, becomes the landlord of the defaulting tenant. As such, he has recourse to the demised premises in the sense that he can pursue a forfeiture claim against that tenant. At the same time, he himself becomes tenant of the (now) head landlord. (Where the lease is a new tenancy, it is always possible that the claimant will be a former tenant who is, at the time, liable to the landlord under the terms of an authorised guarantee agreement.)

The problem that this potentially causes for the landlord who has served the section 17 notice is a two-fold one. First, he is deprived of the ability to forfeit the occupational lease himself and re-let the premises. Secondly, the claimant may no longer be a financially sound entity. If the claimant then proceeds to forfeit the occupational lease, the landlord will be left with remedies only against the claimant. Service of a section 17 notice is therefore tantamount to inviting the recipient to become your tenant.

Section 19 of the 1995 Act goes on to provide that the overriding lease is to be granted for the remainder of the term of the lease that it overrides, plus three days. It is to contain the same covenants as that lease, subject to any modifications agreed to by the claimant and the landlord. Supplementary provisions are to be found in section 20 of the 1995 Act, including provisions that effectively dispense with the requirement for a mortgagee's consent where the landlord's interest is mortgaged or charged.

At least two practical problems arise. What is the position if the relevant tenancy is, in fact, a continuation tenancy under the Landlord and Tenant Act 1954? How is the term of the overriding lease to be calculated? And what is the position if the landlord is himself a tenant and requires the consent of the superior landlord for the grant of derivative interests? Neither section affords assistance here.

What are the disadvantages for the former tenant (or former guarantor) who claims an overriding lease? He will have to pay the landlord's reasonable costs "of and incidental to the grant of" the overriding lease. This may well involve the landlord's surveyors' fees in addition to those of the landlord's solicitors. Furthermore, there is no exemption from stamp duty in the case of the overriding lease. He may well become liable to provide services to the tenant under the lease that is overridden, and on an assignment of the overriding lease – if it is a new tenancy – he may well have to enter into an AGA. He will not enjoy the protection of Part II of the Landlord and Tenant Act 1954 because he will not normally be in occupation of any part of the demised premises for the purposes of a business.

However, a more real problem arises where a former tenant, who is an assignee, has met the burden of a fixed charge not by making payment to the landlord pursuant to a section 17 notice served upon him but rather as a result of a successful indemnity claim brought by his own assignor.

The decision of the High Court in *M W Kellogg Limited* v *Tobin* [1999] L & TR 513 makes it clear that section 17 does not oblige the assignor in these circumstances to serve a notice under that section on his assignee as a condition of pursuing the indemnity claim. It follows that the assignee has no entitlement to an overriding lease, despite the fact that he has indirectly met the fixed charge. Is this a point that should be covered expressly by contract in the transfer or assignment of the lease?

FORFEITURE

Forfeiture of the lease remains the landlord's principal remedy when faced with a tenant who has failed to pay his rent or is otherwise in breach of the covenants contained in his lease, notwithstanding that in recessionary times landlords may often be reluctant to resort to this remedy. An express proviso for forfeiture should always be included in the lease, since none will be implied. (It is only on denial of a landlord's title that an implied right to forfeit arises.) Save where the breach of covenant in question is a continuing one, the landlord must ensure that no act of waiver of the right to forfeit has occurred. The generally accepted view is that drafting will not save a landlord in this respect. (See later and in particular *R* v *Paulson* [1921] 1 AC 271 and *Expert Clothing Service and Sales Limited* v *Hillgate House Limited* [1986] Ch 340.)

Forfeiture can presently be achieved either by peaceable re-entry onto the premises or by means of court proceedings for possession. The exact time of forfeiture is governed by the method chosen. Forfeiture determines, at common law, all derivative interests created under the lease. What the landlord must not do is to ignore the many consequences of a completed forfeiture, in particular where the former tenant continues to occupy.

Perhaps the most obvious point to make is that liability for future rent ceases. Any rent due and unpaid at the date of forfeiture is recoverable by the landlord in full and is not subject to apportionment. Distress ceases to be available as a remedy (since the relationship of landlord and tenant has gone). Thereafter, the landlord's claim is for mesne profits for the tenant's use and occupation of the premises as a trespasser.

The general rule seems to be that mesne profits should equate to the ordinary letting value of the premises but that rule can be displaced. In *Ministry of Defence* v *Ashman* [1993] 66 P & C R 195, the tenant had previously enjoyed the benefit of a concessionary rent. The Court of Appeal held that mesne profits should be awarded at the true value of the accommodation to the occupier rather than at its open market value.

Equally obvious is the fact that the covenants in the lease cease to run. Where there are continuing breaches of those covenants, it will not be open to the landlord, for instance, to apply to the court for injunctive relief based upon them. Likewise, the landlord may well have to find some basis in tort for any claim against the tenant in respect of deterioration of the premises, since the benefit of the tenant's repairing covenant will have been lost.

The ongoing liability of guarantors also terminates, save possibly where the lease makes express provision to the contrary such as the grant of an option in the landlord's favour to require any guarantor to take up a substitute lease. (In this respect, however, see below.)

The decision of the High Court in *G S Fashions Limited* v *B & Q plc* [1995] 1 EGLR 62 sounds one final word of warning for landlords. Where a landlord has issued and served proceedings claiming forfeiture of the lease and seeking an order for possession, it will not be open to the landlord to change his mind about this course of action if the tenant has admitted the breach of covenant and the landlord's entitlement to forfeit.

The Law Commission has since 1985 recommended reform of the law of forfeiture by means of codification. There is no indication at present of when Parliament might consider reform, despite the existence of a draft

Termination of Tenancies Bill published by the Law Commission in 1994.

GROUP SHARING

A landlord may be asked by the proposed tenant, at the stage of lease negotiation, to agree to a "group sharing" provision, notwithstanding that the lease is intended to contain an absolute prohibition on sharing or parting with possession or occupation of the demised premises, otherwise than by means of an assignment or underletting of the whole. The purpose of this is to permit a tenant company to share occupation of the demised premises with a company or companies within the group of companies of which it is a member. This can often provide the tenant with some compensation for an absolute restriction on underlettings of part.

The first point to consider is whether this arrangement is to be personal to a named tenant company. (This is the safer course for a landlord.) It is then important to choose a satisfactory definition of "group company". Those taken from taxation legislation can be too wide for this purpose. It is preferable to refer to section 42(1) of the Landlord and Tenant Act 1954. This provides as follows:

> *"For the purposes of this section two bodies corporate shall be taken to be members of a group if and only if one is a subsidiary of the other or both are subsidiaries of a third body corporate.*
>
> *In this subsection "subsidiary" has the meaning given by section 736 of the Companies Act 1985".*

Further express safeguards for the landlord are advisable:

- The arrangement should automatically come to an end when the group relationship ceases.
- No tenancy should at any time be created.
- Written notice of the arrangement, and of its termination, should be given to the landlord.
- A maximum number of separate occupancies should be imposed.

Additional controls may be necessary where the landlord himself is in occupation of other premises in the same building, e.g. in relation to business competition.

GUARANTORS

The decision by Neuberger J in *Active Estates Limited* v *Parness* [2002] 3 EGLR 13 suggests that some aspects of present drafting practice in relation to a guarantor's obligations may be defective. If this is so, then it should perhaps have been apparent some six years earlier when the House of Lords decided the leading case in this area.

Let us look at present drafting practice. Leases commonly purport to grant the landlord the right to require the guarantor to take up a "substitute" lease in some or all of the following instances:

1 Disclaimer by a liquidator or a trustee in bankruptcy or by the Crown.

2 Forfeiture of the lease.

3 Acceptance of a surrender by the landlord (e.g. from a liquidator).

4 The tenant for any reason ceasing to exist as a legal entity.

(The rights are conferred upon the landlord in the lease by creation of a specific put option in his favour.)

Additionally, the guarantor is usually required to covenant with the landlord that in the event of the landlord becoming entitled to exercise the put option but electing not to do so, the guarantor will pay the equivalent of the rent for the demised premises until the landlord is able to re-let them.

There are quite sound commercial reasons for a landlord to seek such rights as against the guarantor. If the guarantor is properly to be viewed as a "shadow" tenant with parallel liability, then in any of these instances, the landlord will wish to pull the guarantor in from the shadows and cause him to stand in the shoes of the actual tenant for the residue of the original term.

It has generally been accepted that such rights subsist as part of a collateral bargain between the landlord and the guarantor – without which the landlord would probably not have agreed to grant the lease – but now it is questionable how far such rights will survive in the event of various instances of premature determination of the lease.

In particular, quite distinct differences apply in the cases of disclaimer from those that apply in the other three instances, especially forfeiture. In part this is because of the provisions of sections 178 and 315 of the Insolvency Act 1986, and in part because of the untidy state of the law relating to forfeiture of leases. (The Law Commission, as we have seen, has long recommended codification and simplification of the law.)

Disclaimer of the lease

The relevant principles to be extracted from the judgment of Lord Nicholls in *Hindcastle Limited* v *Barbara Attenborough Associates Limited* [1997] AC 70 (which is the leading case, albeit concerned with liability on the part of a third party to pay rent rather than to take up a "substitute" lease) are these:

- Where only the landlord and the tenant are involved, all future liabilities – each to the other – are extinguished by the disclaimer. The lease terminates for all purposes.
- Where third parties are involved, the future liability of the insolvent tenant in possession and the landlord

– each to the other – are extinguished by the disclaimer. The lease again terminates, but for the purpose of perpetuating the rights and liabilities of the landlord and the third parties, it is deemed by statute to continue in being.

- This latter state of affairs comes to an end if a vesting order is made or the landlord re-takes possession. Lord Nicholls said

> *"If no vesting order is made and the landlord takes possession, the liabilities of other persons to pay the rent and perform the tenant's other covenants will come to an end as far as the future is concerned. If the landlord acts in this way, he is no longer the involuntary recipient of a disclaimed lease. By his own act of taking possession he has demonstrated that he regards the lease as ended for all purposes. His conduct is inconsistent with there being a continuing liability on others to perform the tenant covenants in the lease. He cannot have possession of the property and at the same time claim rent for the property from others."*

There will always be the risk for a landlord that he acts in such a way that he unwittingly re-takes possession at some point following disclaimer. Therefore, until now landlords negotiating leases have tended to be advised not to rely upon the position under the general law but rather to continue to impose a contractual liability on the guarantor in the lease to take up a "substitute" lease, if required to do so, where disclaimer occurs. (The landlord is in a position legally to grant the "substitute" lease because the disclaimer – as seen above – will already have terminated the original lease for this purpose.)

The decision in the present case by Neuberger J confirms that while the liability of a guarantor, following disclaimer, to take up a "substitute" lease survives disclaimer, it also comes to an end on the landlord re-taking possession. The judge gave several convincing reasons why the principle stated by Lord Nicholls should apply in this instance also. In particular, he stated *"Re-taking possession after disclaimer is scarcely consistent with requiring a new lease to be taken by the guarantor"*.

A landlord faced with disclaimer occurring now should serve the notice exercising the put option even more speedily than before, where there is little likelihood of re-letting in the open market on better terms.

Forfeiture of the lease

Here, other considerations apply. There is no interference from the Insolvency Act 1986. It is also an established principle of landlord and tenant law that forfeiture operates to terminate the future liability of all parties to a lease.

However, the water is somewhat muddied. This is because there can be doubt in many instances as to the actual moment of forfeiture. It is clear from decided authorities that forfeiture does not occur on the issue of proceedings for possession. (This is simply treated as an election by the landlord to proceed to forfeit the lease on the ground of the alleged breach.) Rather, it occurs on enforcement of the order for possession, at which time also the right to apply for relief is lost.

On the other hand, where the landlord resorts to peaceable re-entry, forfeiture occurs at the time of re-entry. But there still remains a limbo period – "a half twilight" – until the time for an application for relief is treated as having expired.

Neuberger J stated in the present case

> *"If the landlord lawfully re-entered the premises before the lease was disclaimed there can be no real doubt but that his right to enforce [the "substitute" lease provision] would (subject to any question of relief from forfeiture) be lost".*

This seems to be saying that such a provision cannot survive a *completed* forfeiture – as compared to a disclaimer – of the lease unless there is a successful application for relief resulting in the lease subsequently being restored. But is it safe to assume that, where the landlord resorts to proceedings, rather than peaceable re-entry, such a provision does survive until the possession order is made or even until it is enforced? (It would certainly be foolish to assume that it survives forfeiture by peaceable re-entry.)

If it does so survive, then service of the relevant notice on the guarantor exercises the put option and a binding agreement for lease arises. The law will imply the usual obligation for completion "within a reasonable time". If the landlord is forced to grant the "substitute" lease before forfeiture of the original lease is complete, then the "substitute" lease must amount to an overriding lease. The landlord then cannot be in a position to complete the forfeiture. A very untidy situation results.

Perhaps the better drafting approach now is to deal with forfeiture separately from disclaimer, granting a distinct put option to the landlord exercisable on proceedings for forfeiture and possession being issued. The provisions would have to be drafted so as to ensure that completion of the grant of the "substitute" lease is postponed until forfeiture is complete, and is conditional upon that.

Surrender of the lease

It must surely now be assumed that a completed surrender also terminates the right of the landlord to have a "substitute" lease taken up. The effect of surrender is to terminate all future rights and liabilities of the parties to the lease. The courts have held that the effect is sufficiently immediate so as to wipe out even "dying breath" liabilities. (See below.) Against that, the issue is probably an academic one in that such a provision will inevitably be resisted at the stage of lease negotiation, and is probably not that necessary for a landlord's protection.

The tenant ceasing to exist as a legal entity

It is questionable to what extent a provision such as this is necessary for the protection of the landlord. If the tenant is an individual who dies, liability for payment of the rent and performance of the tenant's covenants in any event devolves upon his personal representatives. If a limited company is dissolved or otherwise removed from the register of companies, the lease will vest as *bona vacantia* and it will usually be possible to secure a disclaimer by the Crown. This will make the put option in the landlord's favour exercisable against the guarantor.

In conclusion, therefore, the crucial instances are disclaimer and forfeiture. The collateral obligations from the guarantor will clearly survive disclaimer and, provided that the landlord avoids re-taking possession and as long as no vesting order is made, it should be possible for the landlord in this instance to procure the completion of a "substitute" lease by the guarantor.

The position is far less clear in the case of forfeiture. If the landlord forfeits by peaceable re-entry, it is difficult to see how the put option survives save possibly where there is a successful application for relief. (Would there then be any need for the exercise of the option?) In the event that the landlord resorts instead to proceedings, then possibly the option continues to be exercisable up to the point of enforcement of the order for possession, if the guarantee provisions in the lease are appropriately worded.

(If we consider, by way of analogy, the permitted content of an authorised guarantee agreement, it is interesting to note that the draftsman of the Landlord and Tenant (Covenants) Act 1995 in section 16 limited the ability of the landlord to require a "substitute" lease to be taken up to instances of disclaimer only. Possibly the draftsman knew best.)

Perhaps we therefore have to accept that where premature determination is brought about by the landlord himself, he cannot both have his cake and eat it.

HEADS OF TERMS

Conventionally, when a commercial letting has been negotiated, heads of terms will be circulated to the parties and their respective advisers by the landlord's surveyor. They are intended to reflect the subject to contract terms agreed with the tenant's surveyor, and to provide a basis for the preparation of the draft lease by the landlord's solicitor. In practice, heads of terms often tend to be skeletal, on the assumption that the flesh will be provided by the parties' solicitors.

There are several drawbacks to this approach. The landlord's solicitor will often need to refer back to his client's surveyor for clarification of what was negotiated, or risk putting his own interpretation on the heads of terms. The tenant's solicitor may well have a similar problem when presented with the draft lease. The exercise of amending and approving the draft then inevitably exposes some *lacunae* in the negotiations. That may well involve a further meeting or discussion between the respective surveyors, and possibly revised heads of terms. Delay and increased costs result.

To illustrate this, assume the letting on an FRI basis for a term of 15 years of a newly constructed stand-alone unit on an industrial estate. Rent reviews are five yearly upwards only. There is to be a tenant's break right exercisable at the expiry of the fifth year of the term. A holding company guarantee is to be provided.

In the box below there are set out some traditional heads of terms in short form, omitting only reference to the identity of the proposed parties and their respective advisers.

TRADITIONAL HEADS OF TERMS

PREMISES:	**Unit A, Longwater Lane, Midtown.**
TERM:	**15 years**
BREAK RIGHT:	**Tenant's conditional at the end of the fifth year**
RENT:	**£12.75 per square metre per annum exclusive**
RENT REVIEW:	**Five yearly upwards only**
REPAIR:	**Full repairing and insuring**
ALIENATION:	**Assignment (with AGA) and subletting of the whole**
USER:	**Industrial**
ALTERATIONS:	**Internal non-structural only and with prior consent**
GUARANTEE:	**Parent company**
COSTS:	**Tenant pays both parties**

Let us now consider, under the same headings, the further issues that potentially arise and that which will need to be resolved.

Premises: The extent of the total intended demise should be shown by means of a suitable plan, which in turn will enable conveyancing searches to be put in hand immediately, if the results of recent searches are not being provided by the landlord's solicitor. Where easements for access, off-site parking and services etc. will need to be granted, the servient land should also be shown. Finally, an architect's drawing showing the floor area of the unit and sufficient to allow approximate measurements to be taken should accompany the heads of terms.

Term: The heads of terms should identify the date from which the term of the lease is to be computed.

Break Right: Is this to be personal to the original tenant? Is it to be conditional? What period of notice is required? Is the right linked to rent review?

Rent: There should be provision for a joint measuring exercise of the floor area of the unit to be conducted in accordance with the current edition of the *RICS Guide to Measuring Practice*. How will the rent commencement date be identified?

Rent Review: Are these to take place at the expiry of the fifth and tenth years only or will there be provision for a penultimate day of the term review? Is there to be a rent review specification? What is the length of the notional term? Will the independent valuer act as expert or arbitrator?

Repair and Insurance: Who will be responsible for wants of repair arising out of design or construction defects? Is there a latent defects policy in force? Will collateral warranties be provided? Are there any facilities used in common requiring the imposition of a service charge by the landlord? If so, on what basis will liability be apportioned? Can the identity of the buildings insurer be agreed and credit given for commission or agency payments received? Who will bear the risk of damage resulting from acts of terrorism?

Alienation: Will there simply be a qualified covenant against assignment, or are express tests to be imposed? Is the AGA requirement to be automatic or qualified by a test of reasonableness? Is there a minimum rent level to be achieved on a subletting of the whole? Will group sharing be permitted and if so what is the maximum number of occupancies?

User: This should be specified more closely, and possibly by reference to the current Town and Country Planning (Use Classes) Order.

Alterations: How are the tenant's fitting out works to be dealt with? Will a simultaneous Licence for Alterations be required? What are the re-instatement requirements at the expiry of the lease? Can minor works be carried out without the requirement for consent?

Guarantee: The guarantor company should be identified by name and company registration number. Is there any limit in time or other cap to the guarantee? Is the guarantee to extend to underwriting performance of any AGA?

Costs: Is this limited to legal costs? Can they be estimated?

Ideally, the lease should be no more than the mechanical means by which effect is given contractually to the terms which the parties have agreed should govern the letting, and it should involve a minimum of negotiation. There is much that any commercial lease should contain, if it is not to be unreliable or defective. The necessary wording, however, is largely standard. Provisions particular to the letting in hand can more readily be drafted and approved if the points are negotiated in full at the heads of terms stage by the parties respective agents and solicitors, and the subject to contract agreement then recorded.

Such a shift of emphasis from the preparation and approval of the draft lease to the negotiation of the heads of terms must inevitably involve the parties' solicitors at a stage when it is presently rare for them to be involved. Should such a suggestion be criticised? It is generally accepted that close collaboration between surveyor and solicitor on any letting transaction produces the best result. For that collaboration to commence at the outset must be to the advantage of the client. The time spent by the solicitor at this early stage will in most cases be offset by the saving in time at the lease negotiation stage. In all probability there will be no increased cost to the client, be it landlord or tenant, and completion of the lease should be achieved that much earlier.

INSURANCE

A landlord will inevitably seek to place his buildings insurance with an insurer where there is an agency or commission arrangement in place. He will then expect to retain any premium discount allowed or commission paid in respect of the annual premium, charging the gross amount to the tenant or tenants. (In the alternative, the commission may be retained by his insurance brokers as a payment for their services.) Is a landlord entitled to do this in the absence of some express provision to that effect in the lease?

The courts have shown an unwillingness to imply tests of reasonableness into provisions for re-imbursement of insurance premiums by tenants. In *Havenridge* v *Boston Dyers Limited* [1994] 2 EGLR 73 the Court of Appeal declined to do so where the tenant had covenanted to pay to the landlord "all sums as the Lessor shall from time to time properly expend or pay to any insurance company". They did however, hold that the word "properly" imported a test of good faith, i.e. was the money paid in the ordinary course of business between the insurer and the landlord?

In *Berrycroft Management Co Limited* v *Sinclair Gardens Investments (Kensington) Limited* [1997] 1 EGLR 47 the landlord enjoyed freedom under the leases to nominate both the insurer and the agency through which the insurance was to be placed. The Court of Appeal was unwilling to imply any terms which would restrict the landlord's freedom when premiums increased dramatically on a change of insurer. It was, in the appeal judges' view, down to the parties to deal expressly with this.

A more recent first instance decision provides further guidance. In *Williams* v *Southwark London Borough Council* [2000] EGCS 44, commission amounting to about £1.3 million was involved. The council was landlord of some 6,000 long leasehold flats disposed of under the "right to buy" provisions in the Housing Act 1985. (This was a test case.) The leases obliged the council to insure and the lessees to reimburse the premiums incurred each year.

In 1995 the council had entered into an agreement with Zurich for the insurance of the buildings in question. Under that agreement, the landlord accepted the obligation to carry out local claims handling on behalf of Zurich. The agreement entitled the landlord to a discount of 25% on the amount of the gross premium. This was made up of a 5% five year loyalty bonus and a 20% fee for the services the council had agreed to provide. The council had charged the full amount of the premium to the lessees.

For the purpose of the case it was accepted that this was a valid agreement and one that the council was properly entitled to enter into. It was also accepted that the council owed no fiduciary duty to the lessees.

It was conceded that the 5% loyalty commission should have been passed on to the lessees. However, Lightman J held that the balance properly belonged to the council. It was not, in fact or in law, a rebate or deduction from the premium payable but rather a payment for services. (He went on to say that if he were wrong on the latter point, then the council would still have been entitled under the lease to pass on to the lessees the actual cost of the claims handling involved.)

There are lessons to be learnt from this decision when a form of lease is being settled. What deductions (if any) will the insurers allow to be made from the gross premium payable? What sums (if any) will the insurers pay to the landlord for placing the insurance? What is the nature of the payment or deduction?

If it reflects an agency or loyalty commission, there must be doubt as to the landlord's entitlement to retain it in the absence of some express provision. To the extent that it amounts to a consideration for management services to be performed by the landlord for the insurer, it may well belong to the landlord but the terms of the lease should in either case state what the parties intend.

LANDLORD AND TENANT ACT 1954

Part II of the Landlord and Tenant Act 1954 is presently undergoing reform. (This has been a long drawn out process.) The proposed changes largely reflect recommendations made by the Law Commission in 1992. Reform is being implemented by means of a Regulatory Reform Order, rather than primary legislation, relying upon the provisions of the Regulatory Reform Act 2001. This new procedure – supposedly a fast-track procedure – is not proving to be without its difficulties.

A draft Order entitled *Draft Statutory Instrument: The Regulatory Reform (Business Tenancies)(England and Wales) Order 2003* was laid before parliament in July 2002. The Government's intention was that the changes would come into effect six months after the making of the Order, so as to allow supporting notice regulations and changes to the Civil Procedure Rules to be made. By the end of 2002, progress ground to a halt because the House of Lords Select Committee recommended in November that the contracting out proposals (contained in Articles 21 and 22 and Schedules 1 to 4 of the draft Order) should be omitted, and any necessary consequential amendments made. The view of the Committee was that those particular reforms were not suited to this procedure, in that they result in protection being lost to tenants. (No such concern was expressed by the House of Commons Select Committee.)

The Government subsequently undertook research in a limited number of county courts into the question why (apparently) about 20% of applications for contracting out orders are rejected and the extent to which this is due to mere procedural errors. (Anecdotal evidence suggests that few applications are refused on substantive grounds.) A report on the results of that research is expected to be put to the two Parliamentary committees in the autumn of 2003. If the Order is then made, the changes would have effect by the late spring of 2004.

Subject to that, here is a brief summary of the proposed changes.

Contracting out

There will be a completely new procedure to follow in order to ensure that a lease is "contracted out" of the continuation and renewal provisions of the 1954 Act. This will require, first, a notice in prescribed form containing a "health warning" to be served on the tenant before the tenant, in the words of the new section 38, *"...enters into the tenancy to which it applies, or (if earlier) becomes contractually bound to do so..."*

The second requirement is that *either* not less than 14 days must elapse before the time when the tenant enters into the tenancy/agreement for tenancy; *or* the tenant must before that time make a statutory declaration in a prescribed form setting out that he understands the implications of his actions. Thirdly, a reference to the notice and (if applicable) the statutory declaration must be contained in, or endorsed on, the tenancy. Finally the agreement to exclude the provisions of sections 24 to 28 of the Act must be contained in or endorsed upon the instrument creating the tenancy, as at present.

Surrenders

In relation to surrenders, the distinction between an immediate surrender and an agreement for a future surrender will be perpetuated. An immediate surrender will remain a perfectly valid method of terminating a tenancy protected by the Act. An agreement to surrender will not. Although there will no longer be any requirement for such agreements to be authorised by the court, the agreement to be valid must comply with similar requirements to those set out above in relation to agreements to contract out of the Act.

Section 25 notices

Section 25 notices, where the landlord is not opposing the grant of new tenancy, will also have to set out the landlord's proposals for the property to be comprised in the new tenancy, the rent to be payable and the other terms of the new tenancy. The notice will also have to contain a "health warning" in an attempt to ensure that tenants do not feel that they have no choice but to accept the landlord's proposals. The requirement for a tenant's counter-notice to be served following a section 25 notice will be abolished.

Where there is a split reversion, it will be open to the landlords to serve separate notices relating to the individual parts of the premises. Likewise the tenant will be able to serve separate requests.

Section 26 requests

Section 26 requests will remain much as now. Also retained will be the requirement for a landlord to serve a counter-notice stating whether he intends to oppose renewal and, if so, upon what ground or grounds. Failure to do so will prevent the landlord from opposing or seeking an order terminating the tenancy. The so-called "pre-emptive strike" will be abolished. (See below.)

Section 27 notices

Section 27(1) of the Act provides that a tenant under a fixed contractual term who wishes to prevent a continuation tenancy arising under section 24 of the Act, and consequent liability for performance of the covenants during that tenancy, may serve a minimum of three months' written notice to that effect on his immediate landlord. This statutory provision was considered by the Court of Appeal in *Esselte* v *Pearl Assurance plc* [1997] 1 EGLR 73. There it was held that if a tenant ceases business occupation at or before the end of a fixed contractual term the Act no longer applies, with the result that no continuation tenancy arises and no notice is required. An amendment to the section will give statutory effect to the *Esselte* decision, so providing tenants with an alternative to serving a section 27(1) notice.

Section 27(2) of the Act allows for service of a similar notice either during the final three months of the contractual term or after the continuation tenancy arises. This will be amended to remove the requirement that such a notice expires on a quarter day. Provision is also made for apportionment of rent in this context.

Section 40 notices

Section 40 of the Act enables one party to a business tenancy to seek information from the other by written notice at any time during the last two years of the contractual term. This is an essential step before starting the procedure to renew or terminate the tenancy. Revised statutory provisions will require the recipient of such a notice to reply in writing within a month, and to keep the information up-to-date for six months. A claim in damages for breach of statutory duty will become available where there is a failure to comply with such a notice. Provision is made for the transfer of obligations and benefits on an assignment of the lease or the reversion.

Renewal applications

In future both parties will be able to apply to the court, either for an order for the grant of a new lease or, in the case of landlords, for an order for termination of the tenancy. At present, it is only the tenant who can instigate court proceedings and can therefore dictate when an application is made and served. The initial deadline for the court application is extended to the date specified in the landlord's section 25 notice, or the day before the date specified in the tenant's section 26 request. Further extensions will be possible by agreement between the parties, so avoiding the need for a court application in many cases.

Interim rent

The pre-emptive strike is abolished. Two new provisions in section 24A will achieve this. First, either party may apply for an interim rent. Secondly, interim rent will be payable from the earliest date for termination of the tenancy which could have been specified in the landlord's section 25 notice or the tenant's section 26 request, irrespective of which party applies for renewal or interim rent.

The present provisions of section 24A of the Act ensure that an interim rent falls below the level of open market value. This principle of valuation will continue where the renewal application is opposed (as defined). However, where renewal is uncontested, the interim rent will simply be the same as the rent for the new renewed tenancy. There are complex, but limited, exceptions to this new principle that are designed to allow an adjustment if unfairness would result. The court will also now have to have regard to the rent payable under any sub-tenancy of part of the premises.

Contol of the business

The Act has always contained anomalies in the way it treats business entities that are, in effect, the *alter ego* of each other. For example, where a tenant is an individual and subsequently forms a company to carry on his business, the Act may operate so as to deprive him of his security of tenure. Similarly, a company landlord may not oppose renewal so as to allow the controlling shareholder to occupy the premises.

The present proposal is to extend the scope of the Act so as to cover more situations where a party organises his affairs so that his property and his business are in separate ownership. In this way, the effect of the Act will generally be neutral when decisions are made as to whether to incorporate a business or vest property in a company. There is however no intention that the "veil of incorporation" should be lifted generally. It will still remain the case, for instance, that it is only the existing tenant who can apply for a new tenancy; this right will not pass to a company controlled by him.

Further changes

The tenant will now have a claim for compensation where there has been misrepresentation or concealment of materials facts by the landlord in cases where he has quit the premises after failing to apply for a renewal, or after withdrawing an application for renewal, in addition to cases where the application has gone to trial. In relation to compensation for disturbance, the changes are largely intended to rule out anomalies. The maximum length of term that the court can impose is extended from 14 to 15 years.

Retrospective effect

None of the changes will be retrospective and transitional provisions will achieve this. There will, for a time therefore, be a dual regime in force.

LEGAL COSTS

The Costs of Leases Act 1958 relieved tenants from the obligation, albeit one of conveyancing practice and custom only, of paying the fees of the landlord's solicitor on the grant of a lease. (At that time, the fees would have been scale fees.) The effect of section 1 of the Act is that there can be no liability on either party to a lease to pay the other's costs in the absence of an agreement in writing to do so.

Where it has been agreed in negotiations that the tenant is to pay the landlord's costs in connection with the grant of a lease, the landlord will insist upon a covenant in the lease and a similar provision in any agreement for lease. To cover the possibility of the matter not proceeding, the landlord's solicitor will inevitably also seek an unqualified undertaking from the tenant's solicitor to be responsible for those costs in any event. A prudent tenant will seek to limit this to circumstances in which he withdraws for reasons unrelated to the negotiated terms.

The strict position differs on lease renewal against the background of the Landlord and Tenant Act 1954. In *Cairnplace Limited* v *CBL (Property Investment) Co Limited* [1984] 1 WLR 696 the Court of Appeal declined to carry over from the expired lease – as part of the "other terms" under section 35 of the Act – a provision for payment by the tenant of the landlord's costs in connection with the grant of the renewal lease. It was not a correct exercise of judicial discretion to use the wide power conferred by section 35 to deprive the tenant of the protection conferred by a later Act, namely the Costs of Leases Act 1958.

In practice, most landlords are probably successful, as a matter of negotiation in non-contested cases, in persuading the tenant to pay their legal costs on lease renewal.

(Be conscious that an agreement in a lease by the tenant to pay the landlord's cost in relation to the tenant's application for a new tenancy will be void. It amounts to the imposition of a penalty for the purposes of section 38(1) of the Act. See *Stevenson & Rush (Holdings) Limited* v *Langdon* [1979] 1 EGLR 72.)

A landlord will also incur legal costs (a) where a tenant applies for consent under the lease, and (b) on taking steps to enforce the covenants given in the lease by the tenant and any surety. (This can include the costs of a superior landlord.) The lease will inevitably contain an express covenant by the tenant to pay these on an indemnity basis in any event.

MODEL LEASE CLAUSES

The benefits of standardisation, in whole or part, of legal documents in common use have long been recognised. One of the more compelling reasons today for introducing standard forms is the saving involved in professional time, during the drafting and negotiating stages, and the consequential reduction in fees. Equally well recognised, however, are the difficulties of devising forms that are capable of wide acceptance.

The British Property Federation (BPF) has consistently involved itself in the move towards standardisation, initially with the production of a series of construction collateral warranties and then its own form of short-term commercial lease. (See below.) It has also supported the City of London Law Society in producing a comprehensive set of commercial property standard enquires.

In 2000, the BPF joined with the British Council for Offices (BCO) to produce a set of model clauses for use in commercial leases. A consultation document was published in June 2000 by the two bodies setting out a number of draft lease clauses, together with a summary and a detailed commentary. Responses to the consultation paper were subsequently analysed by the working party involved. In February 2003 the two bodies published a final document entitled *BPF & BCO Model Clauses for an FRI Office Lease of Whole.*

(It should be borne in mind, of course, that in the meantime the second edition of the Code of Practice for Commercial Leases was published, and the BPF in particular has supported later moves aimed at encouraging acceptance of its provisions by the commercial property industry. The working party has clearly paid considerable attention to those provisions.)

The model clauses are drafted on the basis of a 15-year FRI office lease of a whole building without service charge provisions but the intention is that they should be transferable to other property market sectors. At the start of the consultation exercise, Richard Kauntze of the BCO was quoted as saying *"[They] focus on those areas of a transaction where the parties will almost always meet at the middle point"*.

The document argues that standard terms, provided that they are fair, can ease the negotiation process and allow the parties to concentrate on "key commercial terms". The BPF and the BCO both accept that the circumstances within the property market would never be typical enough to make the concept of a "Standard FRI Lease" a realistic goal. But they contend that many elements within an FRI lease are capable of being standardised. The thinking is that if these tend to cover matters unlikely to prove to be "deal-breakers", the parties might as well agree their position in advance by accepting the model clauses. (This might well be within the heads of terms on a lease negotiation.)

The whole document may now be freely downloaded from www.bpf.org.uk/publications. The conditions of use provide that the whole or any part of it may be used unchanged without charge, provided the user acknowledges that its use is with the consent of the BPF and the BCO.

The initiative is an important one for several reasons:

- It is likely to gain wide support from within the commercial property industry.

- There has been lengthy and extensive consultation and discussion.

- The impact of the model clauses – if they do gain acceptance – will be over a much wider area than that of the BPF's form of short-term commercial lease.
- Standardisation of legal documentation continues to be a current issue.
- The model clauses raise a number of issues in the context of "flexible leases" which need to be considered.
- They may well serve as a benchmark from which to judge specific provisions within individual precedent forms; and from which to assess the acceptability of draft leases offered for approval.

Plain English tends to be used throughout. There is an initial summary of the model clauses and an extremely comprehensive commentary that should be read in conjunction with the model clauses themselves.

Paying rent

These provisions are largely without controversy, as might be imagined. The only payments reserved as rent (with the perceived advantages of distress being available and no section 146 notice being required on forfeiture) are the Principal Rent and the Insurance Rent together with VAT chargeable on either. While most tenants will accept this, many object to distress being available to a landlord in respect of other fluctuating sums, the amount of which may be in dispute. The commentary acknowledges this.

The Principal Rent is payable quarterly in advance on the conventional quarter days. The Insurance Rent is payable within ten business days after written demand.

The commentary recommends that the definition of "Insurance Rent" should include the cost of insurance valuations provided they are commissioned no more frequently than once in every three years. As subsequently defined this expression goes much further in relation to professional fees in this context.

Rights of legal and equitable set-off are understandably excluded. (The Court of Appeal confirmed in *Unchained Growth III plc* v *Granby Village (Manchester) Management Co Limited* [2000] 1 WLR 739 that such an anti-set off clause in a lease is not caught by the Unfair Contract Terms Act 1977.)

Deliberately, no automated method of payment is prescribed in the case of the Principal Rent. (That alone would raise an objection from most commercial landlords, though it should be borne in mind that something of a two-edge sword is involved.) It is always simpler to include such a provision in a lease and then waive it by personal concession where the circumstances justify it.

Sums are expressed to be payable exclusive of VAT. There are conventional provisions for interest (at 3% over base rate) on arrears, including those arising as a result of the landlord refusing to accept payment of rent to avoid waiving a right of forfeiture in respect of a material breach of covenant by the tenant.

Outgoings and services

The tenant pays all outgoings, but is not responsible for any taxes the landlord has to pay.

As this is a lease of the whole of a stand-alone office building, there are no service charge provisions as such included. However, the tenant does have to pay a fair proportion of all the charges for services provided to the premises by the landlord. (In many cases, there will be no such services but a tenant should be aware that if there are, no test of reasonableness will apply in relation to the quantum of the charges.)

Finally, the tenant has to pay "a fair proportion of all reasonable costs and expenses properly incurred by the landlord" in connection with facilities used in common with any adjoining property.

In determining what costs and expenses it is reasonable to spend or incur, the decisions in *Scottish Mutual Assurance plc* v *Jardine Public Relations Limited* [1999] EGCS 43 and *Fluor Daniel Properties Limited* v *Shortlands Investments Limited* [2001] 2 EGLR 103 appear to require the landlord to take into account the respective lengths of the various tenants' leases.

Repair and maintenance

The repairing covenant obliges the tenant (implicitly) to put the premises in repair (to the extent that they are not in that condition) and to keep them in good and substantial repair and condition. There is no attempt made to extend the concept of repair so as to include renewing or rebuilding, though obviously "repair" implicitly involves the renewal of subsidiary parts of the whole.

It may be, in the light of comparatively recent judicial dicta, that in given circumstances the word "condition" may import something more than repair. (In *Welsh* v *Greenwich London Borough Council* [2000] 3 EGLR 41 the Court of Appeal held, in the case of a short residential tenancy agreement, that a reference to "good condition" was intended to mark a separate concept and to make a significant addition to what is conveyed by the word "repair".)

Damage by insured risk is excluded in the usual way.

The commentary suggests that in the case of a new or refurbished building the tenant should be encouraged to use an agreement for lease (rather than the lease itself) as the vehicle to incorporate any agreed elements of protection from the consequences of defective design, materials or workmanship. This seems perfectly appropriate.

The view stated in the commentary is that given the 15-year term, these repairing obligations are consistent with the advice contained in the Code of Practice for Commercial Leases.

Decoration, plant and machinery, day-to-day maintenance and yielding up are dealt with in a conventional way. A clause of the kind approved by the Court of Appeal in *Jervis* v *Harris* [1996] 1 EGLR 78 is included but this is in a form that most tenants would today probably seek to qualify by adding specific safeguards.

Alterations and signs

There is an absolute prohibition on the erection of new structures, on changes in the height, elevation and external design or appearance of the premises and on most structural alterations. (Part I of the Landlord and Tenant Act 1927 is always available, however, to the tenant.)

There is a fully qualified prohibition in the case of other alterations, including certain minor structural alterations. Internal demountable partitioning may be erected, altered and removed without consent, and similarly, certain minor alterations to plant and machinery may be made. There is a fully qualified prohibition in the case of signage visible from the outside of the premises, and an absolute prohibition on window advertisements. (The drafting is complicated.)

Re-instatement is dealt with in the usual way, but most landlords would prefer to see included in addition, a specific right to enter and re-instate at the cost of the tenant in the event of default.

Disposals

The provisions envisage assignment, charging (by means of fixed charge) and underletting of the whole with consent, and underletting of identified parts with consent, but on a contracted out basis and subject to an overall limit on the number of separate occupancies. In every case, consent is expressly not to be unreasonably withheld.

Charges of the whole by means of floating charge are expressed not to require the landlord's consent, if created in the normal course of business in favour of a "Bank of England authorised financial institution".

All underlettings must be at open market rent (as opposed, for instance, to the higher of open market and passing rent) and – if the landlord reasonably so requires – with an acceptable guarantor joined. The usual requirements governing the content of permitted underlettings appear. There is also a group sharing provision, though without all of the safeguards a prudent landlord might wish to see.

Quite detailed provisions are included for the management of the underlettings, and registration requirements are set out in the usual way.

Somewhat surprisingly, no attempt is made to take full advantage of section 19(1A) of the Landlord and Tenant Act 1927 to the extent that it allows the parties to spell out the circumstances in which the landlord will be entitled to withhold consent to an assignment. (Instead, the test of reasonableness applies.)

The commentary suggests that this is unnecessary, as long as the landlord is entitled to act reasonably in withholding consent. (This very much conflicts with the approach of the ABI Working Party in its 1996 Report.) Nevertheless, the commentary then sets out many of the circumstances commonly encountered when full reliance is placed on section 19(1A), including some recommended by the ABI Working Party.

Section 19(1A) is relied upon, however, to enable the parties to specify a limited number of conditions which the landlord has discretion to impose on granting consent to an assignment of the whole.

Where reasonable, the landlord may require a rent deposit, a bank guarantee or a third party guarantee. There is an absolute entitlement to an AGA on each assignment. This does accord with the recommendation of the ABI Working Party, but tends to run counter to the approach set out in the Code of Practice on Commercial Leases.

There is also an absolute entitlement to a parallel guarantee, by the outgoing tenant's guarantor, of compliance with the terms of the AGA. (The advance requirement for a parallel guarantee, as the commentary acknowledges, has yet to withstand judicial scrutiny, and a severability clause may be desirable.)

Unpaid rents must be paid prior to completion of the assignment, and the landlord can impose "such other conditions as may be reasonable in the circumstances".

Further documentation is required simply to be in such form as the landlord reasonably requires. Most tenants would prefer to see a settled form of AGA (and rent deposit deed where appropriate) scheduled to the lease from the outset. Apart from giving contractual certainty, it avoids yet further delay at the time of an assignment.

Insurance

The introduction to the document states

> *"Most of the thinking and all of the consultation on the commentary and the clauses occurred prior to 11th*

September 2001. Clearly the position on insured risks has become more of an issue since then".

The commentary explains the absence of any specific provision in relation to uninsured risks by referring to the lack of any industry wide consensus on the issue. It does, however, refer to the recommendation in the Code of Practice for Commercial Leases that if premises are damaged by uninsured risk, so as to prevent occupation, the tenant should be allowed to terminate the lease unless the landlord agrees to rebuild at its own cost.

The actual insurance provisions are grouped together, adopt the customary approach and are relatively short. They do, however, depend heavily upon definitions, some of which will inevitably fall outside the scope of the present initiative.

The landlord covenants to insure and to re-instate, subject to the usual conditions. The tenant covenants not to vitiate. The commentary makes heavy reference to the general advice contained in the Code of Practice for Commercial Leases in relation to competitive terms and choice of insurer.

Rent suspension is in respect of the Principal Rent only – which would probably not be acceptable to a tenant under a lease requiring on account service charge payments – and will not operate until the rent day following the damage or destruction. A tenant will usually seek to provide for repayment of the appropriate apportioned amount where damage or destruction occurs part way through a rent period. Equally, a prudent tenant will have in mind the need to fit out again following rebuilding or re-instatement. Somewhat unusually, there is an option for open-ended rent suspension.

Neither party is given an express right to determine the lease in the event that re-instatement is frustrated. The landlord has to use reasonable endeavours to ensure that the tenant's interest is noted on the policy (though the commentary acknowledges that the legal effect of noting is unclear).

The provisions are silent in relation to commission earned on the insurance premiums. (As we have seen, the decision in *Williams* v *Southwark London Borough Council* [2000] EGCS 44 demonstrates the need to deal expressly with this.) Likewise, a landlord usually expects the tenant to covenant to pay the amount of any excess on a claim.

Costs

These provisions do not require much comment. The tenant covenants to pay within ten business days of written demand all costs and expenses properly incurred by the landlord in relation to breaches or prospective breaches of covenant, and in relation to applications for consent. In no instance is the cost level qualified by any test of reasonableness. The commentary acknowledges that in a non-breach situation this may not be appropriate.

Rent review

There is an upward-only provision, and review dates need to be stated in express terms.

Perhaps the first point to note is that, perfectly sensibly, no attempt is made to achieve a headline rent. Nor is there reference to "best rent", which wording would allow evidence of the existence of a special bidder in the market to be adduced.

The possibility of the tenant seeking to advance the argument raised in *99 Bishopsgate Limited* v *Prudential Assurance Co Limited* [1985] 273 EG 984 is ruled out. This is achieved by defining the reviewed rent to be that payable after the expiry of any rent free or concessionary rent period that might be negotiated in the open market for the purposes of fitting out. (This is preferable to the use of a "fitted out" assumption for a number of reasons.)

The length of the hypothetical lease is equal to the unexpired residue of the term of the actual lease, but with a minimum of ten years, and contains provisions for rent review at five yearly intervals

The premises are to be assumed to be in a state and condition ready to be fitted out by the willing tenant There is also an assumption that all of the provisions of the lease have been complied with. (Tenants often contend that if a landlord is in breach of his repairing obligations, for instance, this should be reflected in the reviewed rent. There are, however, arguments against that view.) The remaining assumptions are customary.

There is a disregard of tenant's works (as opposed to any uplift in rent as a result of tenant's works) but the tenant remains exposed in the case of statutory improvements. (See *Forte & Co Limited* v *General Accident Life Assurance Limited* [1986] 2 EGLR 115.) This will generally not be acceptable to tenants. A tenant's amendment would also be required where works have been carried out prior to the commencement of the term.

There is provision for third party determination either by an arbitrator or an expert, but the choice has to be made as part of the lease negotiation.

Time is expressly not of the essence. This is probably in the best interests of each party.

Definitions

A number of relatively standard definitions are offered, without commentary, but these would always need to be tailored to suit the specific precedent being used to draft the remainder of the lease.

In conclusion:

- While the concept is to be highly commended, it may have been wiser to start with a set of principles to be offered for agreement first, as opposed to detailed clauses.
- Where it is agreed to adopt the model clauses, a number of issues within those clauses will still have to be settled.
- Where the model clauses are to be incorporated into a lease of part, the necessary modifications will not always be without controversy.
- A number of "standard" tenant's amendments have been ignored and this is to be regretted.
- Much of the ability that the Landlord and Tenant (Covenants) Act 1995 gives to landlords of commercial premises to control assignments, has largely been ignored.
- Standard rent review provisions will not always be appropriate for lettings in other property market sectors.
- A set of service charge provisions would have been desirable. (These might now be based on the advice contained in new edition of the Guide to Good Practice on Service Charges in Commercial Properties).

NOTICES

It has been recognised judicially on many occasions that, as a general principle of common law, any notice that is tainted by fraud is ineffective. What is perhaps not always appreciated is what constitutes fraud for this purpose.

In *Rous* v *Mitchell* [1991] 1 All ER 676, a number of notices under the Agricultural Holdings Act 1986 alleging breaches of covenant were held to be invalid in that they contained fraudulent statements. The Court of Appeal confirmed the statement made by Lord Herschell in *Derry* v *Peek* (1889) 14 App Cas 337 to the effect that "fraud is proved when it is shown that a false representation has been made (1) knowingly, or (2) without belief in its truth, or (3) recklessly, careless whether it is true or false".

Consider this in the context of notices under section 25 of the Landlord and Tenant Act 1954 opposing renewal of the tenancy and accordingly stating one or more grounds of opposition. If the landlord has stated, for instance, that he intends to demolish or reconstruct the premises comprised within the holding and ultimately this results in the court refusing an order for the grant of a new tenancy, the tenant has a claim for compensation against the landlord under section 55 of the 1954 Act where it is shown that the court was induced to refuse the grant by misrepresentation or the concealment of material facts. The compensation is for the damage or loss sustained by the tenant as the result of the refusal.

This presupposes that the tenant has applied to the court for a new tenancy and sustained that application up to the date of the hearing. What is the position where the tenant has been induced not to apply to the court, or to withdraw his application, and to vacate the premises as a result of the statements made in the section 25 notice? The provisions of section 55 presently will not assist him. The common law may well do so.

It was held by the House of Lords in *Betty's Cafes Limited* v *Phillips Furnishing Stores Limited* [1959] AC 20 that the landlord could succeed in his opposition on the ground that he intended to demolish or reconstruct the premises if he could prove that he held the requisite intention at the date of the hearing of the tenant's application.

But Lord Denning said that the landlord's statement of his grounds of opposition in the earlier notice must still be honest and truthful. Such a notice is intended to be acted on before there is a trial at all. It would be deplorable if a landlord could be allowed to get an advantage by misrepresenting his state of mind or any other fact. He went on to envisage a notice being set aside for a fraudulent misrepresentation with the consequence of the tenancy continuing undetermined, and also the possibility of a claim in damages at common law for fraud.

A landlord should state his intentions in a section 25 notice honestly and scrupulously.

RELEASE FROM LIABILITY

The general principle in the case of new tenancies (for the purposes of the Landlord and Tenant (Covenants) Act 1995) is that tenants are automatically released from future liability in respect of the tenant covenants of the tenancy on an assignment. (The exception is where there has been an excluded assignment.) But there is no automatic release for a landlord on the assignment of a reversion to a new tenancy; only a statutory procedure whereby he can apply to the tenant for a release from future liability in respect of the landlord covenants of the tenancy. (See sections 6 and 8 of the Act.)

(It was held in *BHP Petroleum Great Britain Limited* v *Chesterfield Properties Limited* [2001] 22 EG 155 that the statutory procedure is not available in the case of personal covenants. In that case, the original landlord had given personal covenants to the tenant, in the agreement for lease, to remedy defective building works carried out by the landlord to the demised premises. Following completion of the grant of the lease, it assigned the reversion and then gave notice to the tenant under section 8 of the Act 1995. No counter-notice was served. A number of external glass units in the premises fractured resulting in the service of a dangerous structure notice. When the tenant claimed on the covenants, the original landlord contended that it had achieved a release from liability under the landlord covenants of the tenancy, including liability in respect of the personal covenants contained in the agreement for lease.

The Court of Appeal, affirming the decision and reasoning at first instance of Lightman J, held that a personal covenant could not be a landlord covenant of the tenancy (and so within the statutory procedure for releases). This was because section 28(1) of the Act defined "landlord covenant" as one that fell to be complied with by the landlord, and defined "landlord" for that purpose as "the person for the time being entitled to the reversion". The only landlord bound by the personal covenants was the original landlord.)

The procedure for seeking a release involves the landlord in serving notice in a prescribed form on the tenant either before or within four weeks of the assignment, informing the tenant of the assignment, or proposed assignment, and requesting a release. The landlord achieves a release if the tenant either serves notice consenting to the release or, within four weeks of service of the landlord's notice, fails to serve notice on the landlord objecting to the release. If the tenant serves a notice of objection, the landlord may apply to the county court for a declaration that it is reasonable for the covenants to be released.

Any release obtained is regarded as effective from the date of the assignment in question. Simultaneously, the landlord ceases to be entitled to the benefit of the tenant covenants in the lease. Where the landlord fails to obtain a release, he remains jointly and severally liable with his successor.

What the landlord must appreciate is the drawback this statutory procedure involves in the case of a multi-let development. Section 8 of the Act requires the landlord to deal with *each* tenant individually. Imagine circumstances where a landlord, on disposing of the reversion, secures releases from, say, only 50% of the occupational tenants. Subsequently, his successor becomes insolvent or simply fails to comply with landlord covenants in the leases for the repair of the structure. Those covenants remain enforceable against the former landlord by the tenants from whom a release was not obtained, but they will be the only tenants from whom the former landlord is entitled to recover contributions under the service charge provisions in the leases. A shortfall will result. The landlord might have been better off by not invoking the procedure.

Would contractual terms within the leases providing for an automatic release of the landlord from non-personal covenants on a future assignment of the reversion have been effective? The better view is probably not. Section 25(1) of the Act renders void any agreement relating to the tenancy to the extent that it would have effect to "exclude modify or otherwise frustrate the operation of" any provision of the Act. It seems appropriate to assume that the Act envisages a landlord achieving a future release only by means of the statutory procedure. Contractual terms of this kind would clearly frustrate the operation of that procedure. Against that, an immediate express release is undoubtedly sanctioned by section 26(1)(a) of the Act but a landlord would have to rely upon his ability to negotiate that at the time of disposal.

RENEWAL LEASES

It is accepted commercially that on rent review any uplift in rent attributable to works of improvement carried out by the tenant to the demised premises, at his own cost and other than pursuant to an obligation owed to the landlord, should be disregarded. (Were this not so, the landlord would achieve a windfall and there would be an obvious injustice to the tenant.) There is standard wording in common use to afford this protection to the tenant.

But the standard wording may not always protect the tenant on rent review. It may be open to the court to hold that the works in question do not amount to improvements to the demised premises, but rather they form part of the demised premises. The tenant may then be penalised. This is likely to occur on rent review under a renewal lease.

In *Brett* v *Brett Essex Golf Club Limited* [1986] 1 EGLR 154, the landlord had in 1973 let an area of open land to the tenant subject to a covenant by the tenant to lay out a golf course. The tenant not only laid out an 18-hole course, but also built a clubhouse on the land. Finally, the tenant laid out a 9-hole course on some adjoining land not included in the letting. In 1978, the landlord granted the tenant an entirely new lease which included the land on which the 9-hole course had been formed. The Court of Appeal had to decide whether, on the review of rent under the 1978 lease, the valuer was bound to disregard any effect on rent of the clubhouse and the 9-hole golf course, notwithstanding that they were voluntary improvements carried out by the tenants during the subsistence of the 1973 lease.

The Court of Appeal held, as a matter of construction, that the clubhouse and 9-hole golf course fell outside the wording of the disregard in the 1978 lease. "The demised premises", for the purposes of the rent review clause, were the premises demised by the 1978 lease as they existed at the beginning of the term of that lease. They clearly included the clubhouse and the 9-hole golf course. These items, therefore, could not constitute improvements to "the demised premises." Furthermore, reference to "the tenant" was a reference to the tenant in his capacity as tenant under the 1978 lease.

In *Panther Shop Investments Ltd* v *Keith Pople Ltd* [1987] 1 EGLR 131, again improvements had been carried out by the tenants under an earlier lease. They were held, for the purposes of rent review under a later lease, not to be improvements to the demised premises but to be part of the demised premises.

On the basis of what is quite customary wording in rent review clauses, it seems likely that the grant of a renewal lease will "crystallise" the demised premises in their improved form. What the tenant may still seek to look upon as "improvements" will have become part of the demised premises. It is vital, therefore, on any lease renewal that the tenant asks himself whether any improvements carried out during the subsistence of any earlier lease remain capable of producing an uplift in the rent for the demised premises. If they do, he should seek to have them identified and their impact specifically disregarded on rent review under the renewal lease.

RENT

A lease must fix the amounts of rent payable throughout the term, and those amounts must be certain. Actual figures can be stated, or provision made for the amounts to be ascertained. The lease must also state from what date rent is payable and identify the payment days. If reference is made to "the usual quarter days" in England this will mean March 25th (Lady Day), June 24th (Midsummer Day), September 29th (Michaelmas Day) and December 25th (Christmas Day).

Unless the lease provides that rent is payable in advance, the rule is that it is payable in arrear. There will usually be provisions for payment of interest on unpaid amounts, abatement and suspension and periodic review. There may be reference to rights of legal and equitable set-off. (See below.)

Many landlords will also seek to insist upon the inclusion of provisions for payment of rent by standing order or direct debit. There are distinct administrative advantages for a landlord, and most certainly this approach is likely, in practice, to give the landlord much earlier warning of a tenant running into financial difficulties. However, it can well provide a two-edged sword.

Once payment methods of this kind have been put in place, there is a much greater likelihood of the landlord finding that he has inadvertently waived a right of forfeiture of the lease for some "once and for all" breach of covenant by the tenant of which he can be shown to have actual or constructive knowledge. (This is less likely to occur where the landlord or his agent retains direct control over rent demands and the acceptance of rent.)

The only case to offer a limited degree of comfort to landlords in this respect is *John Lewis Properties Limited* v *Viscount Chelsea* [1993] 2 EGLR 77, where payments of rent were made direct to the landlord's bank by cheque at a time when the landlord had actual knowledge of the alleged breaches of covenant. It was held, *obiter*, by Mummery J (as he then was) – and with some hesitation – that no waiver had occurred. The rent had not been demanded, and in due course repayment of each sum in question had been made by the landlord to the tenant. In all the circumstances, it could not be said that the landlord had "accepted" the rent.

Equally, landlords should not assume that the parties to a lease may choose to contract out of the effect of waiver by providing, for instance, that acts of waiver on the part of the landlord are not to prevent a valid forfeiture of the lease. (See *R* v *Paulson* [1921] 1 AC 271, and also *Expert Clothing Service & Sales Limited* v *Hillgate House Limited* [1985] 2 EGLR 85 where it was accepted as common ground by the Court of Appeal that such clauses are ineffective.) This is largely because the breach of covenant giving rise to the right of forfeiture puts the landlord to an election. He must choose either to treat the lease as continuing or to treat it as at an end.

It is important not to include such provisions in a lease. They are ineffective as a matter of law, and may mislead a landlord or his advisers with costly results.

Strictly, rent is payable in cash at the demised premises on the rent payment day. This is rarely commercially convenient. It remains common for a landlord to agree – expressly or implicitly – to accept payment by cheque. A decision of the Court of Appeal in the context of a residential letting illustrates that the general principles of law relating to payment of a debt by cheque will apply equally to payment of rent in that manner.

In *Day* v *Coltrane* [2003] 30 EG 146 the tenant of a residential flat, who had an assured tenancy under the Housing Act 1988, habitually paid his rent by cheque. He fell into arrears for 11 weeks. His landlord served notice, under section 8 of the Act, of her intention to take proceedings. She then issued proceedings for possession.

The ground pleaded was Ground 8 in Schedule 2 to the Act, namely that both at the date of service of the notice and at the date of the hearing at least eight weeks' rent was outstanding. This is a mandatory ground. In other words, the judge has no discretion if the ground is established. He must make an order for possession. Furthermore, section 9 of the Act prevents the judge from ordering an adjournment of the proceedings in such circumstances.

A few days before the date of the hearing, the tenant sent a cheque to the landlord for the full amount of the arrears. This was accepted, and later cleared on first presentation. At the hearing, the district judge declined to make a possession order, and adjourned the hearing to see whether the cheque would clear. The landlord appealed against the grant of the adjournment. The judge allowed the appeal, and made an order for possession. The tenant appealed to the Court of Appeal.

The Court of Appeal allowed the appeal and set aside the order for possession, holding that the district judge had acted correctly in adjourning the hearing to see whether the cheque cleared. He could not be satisfied at that point in time that the landlord was entitled to possession. He therefore had jurisdiction to adjourn.

The parties had agreed to payment of rent by cheque. There was no reason why the general principles in relation to payment by cheque should not apply to Ground 8 cases. Earlier authorities establish that acceptance of a cheque in payment of a debt suspends the right to sue upon the debt while the cheque is in the process of clearing. If it clears, then the debt is treated as having been paid upon the date when the cheque was delivered.

It was for that reason that the landlord was unable to establish that, at the date of the hearing, at least eight weeks' rent was outstanding.

The appeal judges went on to say that if the cheque had not cleared on first presentation, the order for possession would have to have been made at the adjourned hearing. The "date of the hearing" for the purpose of Ground 8 is then treated as the date of the first hearing and not that of the later adjourned hearing.

This means that a tenant in such a situation can save the day by delivering a cheque to the landlord at any time up to the date of the initial hearing, provided that it subsequently clears on first presentation. Landlords should therefore be conscious of the possible consequences of accepting a cheque at that point, tempting though it might be to collect in the arrears.

RENT DEPOSITS

It is essential to distinguish between rent deposit arrangements in relation to an old tenancy, for the purposes of the Landlord and Tenant (Covenants) Act 1995, and those entered into in relation to a new tenancy. This is important from the point of view of both landlords and tenants.

Where the related lease is an old tenancy, it is unlikely that the benefit and burden of the covenants commonly given in support of the rent deposit arrangements will run with the land. They will not "touch and concern" it. See *Hua Chiao Commercial Bank Limited* v *Chiaphua Industries Limited* [1987] AC 99. Here it was held by the Privy Council that the obligation to repay a rent deposit at the expiry of the term of the lease did not pass from the recipient to his successor as landlord on a transfer of the reversion. Accordingly, the tenant was unable to sue the new landlord for re-payment.

For this reason, it is essential that a rent deposit deed entered into as part of an old tenancy requires the landlord to procure that on the transfer of the reversion, a supplemental deed is entered into containing an acknowledgement by the transferee in favour of the tenant that he is bound by the terms of the original rent deposit deed. The deed should also provide for the rent deposit to be transferred to the new landlord, and for an express release of the old landlord.

Where the lease in question is a new tenancy, the position is more satisfactory from the point of view of the tenant. The effect of section 3 of the 1995 Act is that the benefit and burden of all landlord and tenant covenants of a tenancy will automatically run, save where they are expressed to be personal covenants. By virtue of section 28(1) of the Act, the obligations contained in the rent deposit deed become landlord and tenant covenants of the tenancy. (The rent deposit deed will undoubtedly be a "collateral agreement" for the purpose of that subsection, which then goes on to provide that that "covenant" includes a covenant contained in a collateral agreement.) In such a case, therefore, a successor landlord will always be bound to repay the rent deposit at the end of the term, save where the relevant covenant in the rent deposit deed is expressed to be a personal one.

Undoubtedly, the main concern for a landlord disposing of the reversion upon terms that the rent deposit is transferred to his successor is continuing liability on his covenant to repay the rent deposit to the tenant at some future date. (That concern will possibly even continue despite an express indemnity taken from the successor.) Where the rent deposit arrangement is part of an old tenancy, it is perfectly possible in drafting terms to provide for an automatic release for the landlord on him, say, procuring a fresh covenant for repayment from his successor in the tenant's favour. Statute does not interfere in this respect.

However, there remains a problem in the case of rent deposit arrangements forming part of a new tenancy. The existing landlord will not be automatically released from future liability on his covenants in the rent deposit deed on a transfer of the reversion. He can seek to negotiate a release at the time from the tenant, but this is unlikely to be forthcoming. Alternatively, he could apply formally for a release under sections 6 and 8 of the Act, to avoid remaining liable jointly with the successor landlord, in the hope that the tenant will not object.

What he cannot do is to seek to provide contractually that he will have an automatic release from liability on a future assignment of the reversion. Any such provision must undoubtedly be caught by section 25(1) of the 1995 Act. This renders void any agreement relating to a tenancy to the extent that it would "have effect to exclude modify or otherwise frustrate the operation of any provision" of the Act.

To protect himself, and to achieve a position similar to that possible in the case of rent deposit arrangements forming part of an old tenancy, the landlord will have to ensure that his covenants are expressed to be given by him as personal covenants. As we have seen, the decision of the Court of Appeal in *BHP Petroleum Great Britain Limited* v *Chesterfield Properties Limited* [2001] 22 EG 155 makes it clear that personal covenants do not constitute "landlord covenants" and "tenant covenants" of the tenancy. They are not, therefore, within the statutory release procedure. Equally, they are outside the transmission regime and so an automatic release provision in respect of a personal covenant should not fall foul of the anti-avoidance provisions contained in section 25(1) of the Act.

Finally, it has been suggested that these problems might be avoided by interposing a management company, owned by the landlord, which would hold the deposits and give the necessary covenants for repayment. Such a company could then be sold with the reversion. Whether this would be acceptable to commercial tenants is, perhaps, doubtful. Save in the case of large developments, such a scheme might in any event not warrant the costs involved.

RENT REVIEW

Let us look at one particular aspect of rent review that can still be troublesome today. It is all about incompatibility.

Commercial leases now invariably provide in express terms that the rent reviews will proceed on the basis of a notional lease containing the same terms as the actual lease (albeit, on occasion, with some adjustments.) In the now rare case when a lease is silent on the point, the court will make the assumption that the parties intended a notional letting upon the terms of the actual lease, other than as to quantum of rent.

Once the terms of the notional lease are identified, it may become apparent that some are incompatible with the concept of an open market rent. Perhaps one of the better known cases where this problem arose is *The Law Land Company Limited* v *Consumers' Association Limited* [1980] 2 EGLR 109. The lease had been granted in 1972 to the Consumers' Association, a company limited by guarantee. It contained a covenant by the tenant not without the consent of the landlord to use or permit the premises to be used "other than as offices of the Consumers' Association and its associated organisations". The rent review provisions assumed a notional letting "subject to the provisions of the lease other than the rent thereby reserved".

The question for the Court of Appeal was whether the valuer was entitled to assume, for the purposes of rent review, that the demised premises might be let to anyone, or only to the Consumers' Association or its associated organisations. The answer to this question governed whether or not there could be an open market rent for the demised premises.

The court held that the existence of a named tenant user clause within the notional lease was totally inconsistent with the provisions of the rent review clause that envisaged review to a market rent on the basis of an open market. The lease was a commercial document and a commercial solution to the problem posed had to be found. To give business sense to the rent review clause, the court ordered that the user clause in the notional lease should be left blank, as far as the name of the tenant was concerned, and the name of the notional tenant should ultimately be inserted.

This is an instance of the court making an alteration to the terms of the actual lease, on translating those terms into the terms of the notional lease, to prevent the object of the rent review clause being stultified. But this approach can by no means be guaranteed. It is always up to the draftsman to consider whether any provision within the actual lease – on being carried through to the notional lease – has the potential for raising the argument, on rent review, of incompatibility with the concept of a market rent. If this is the case, then the terms of the notional lease must be adjusted appropriately at the drafting stage.

Equally, the rent review provisions might be deprived of practical effect because of the presence of some physical factor inconsistent with the concept of a market rent.

In the great majority of cases, the starting point for the premises to be valued is that they are the actual demised premises. (The parties are entitled to direct, however, that the rent is to be fixed by reference to notional premises. This they may well choose to do where, for instance, the actual premises have been tailored to the specific needs of the tenant in such a way that they have ceased to be generally marketable, or where the size or nature of construction of the actual premises renders them difficult to compare with other premises in the market. For a recent example, see *Beegas Nominees Limited* v *Decco Limited* [2003] 33 EG 63.)

Whether the premises to be valued are the actual demised premises or some notional ones, it is essential that the draftsman asks himself whether there is anything about the premises which might affect their marketability to such an extent that the tenant is able to contend, on rent review, that there is no open market for them. This is what happened in *Jefferies* v *O'Neill* [1983] 46 P&CR 376.

There, the tenant held the first and second floors of a building under a lease. The adjoining freehold building belonged to the tenant who occupied the two sets of premises together as offices. As a result of alterations to the demised premises, approved of by the landlord, by the time the rent under the lease fell due for review, the only means of access into the demised premises was from the tenant's adjoining freehold building. The tenant sought a declaration that the valuer appointed to determine the rental value of the demised premises should proceed on the basis that there was no open market for the premises, and that the only willing lessee was the tenant. (Such a declaration would obviously deprive the rent review provisions of any real practical effect.)

The judge refused to make the declaration sought. The parties had entered into a lease, after lengthy negotiations, which contained elaborate provisions for fixing an open market rent as between a willing lessor and a willing lessee. To grant the declaration would result in those provisions "being not much more than waste paper". He held that to give commercial efficacy to the lease it was necessary to imply into the rent review clause terms obliging the valuer to disregard the effect on rental value of the existing access arrangements.

This is a further example of the court – albeit by means of what the judge described as "a substantial amendment to the rent review provision itself" – resolving an inconsistency in favour of the notional letting. Ideally, the draftsman should not allow any such inconsistency to arise. The lease itself should contain appropriate provision.

Finally, it is interesting to contrast the approach taken by the court where it is statutory provisions, and not lease terms, that have to be construed. In *J Murphy & Sons Limited* v *Railtrack plc* [2003] L & TR 3 the tenant applied to renew a business lease that granted no right of access to the demised premises. (Access was obtained by the tenant from its adjoining freehold land.) As a preliminary point, the judge held that rental value should be assessed on the basis that the premises were land-locked and that a discount of 40% from open market rental should apply. The landlord appealed to the Court of Appeal contending that (1) the lack of access should be disregarded in addition to the matters referred to in section 34 of the Landlord and Tenant Act 1954 and, in the alternative, (2) the court should include a right of access in the renewal lease.

The Court of Appeal dismissed the appeal, holding as follows: (1) Section 34 was definitive and it was not possible to include additional disregards. Rent review cases (where the court had implied a disregard of the lack of access to give business efficacy to the rent review provisions) were not applicable. They were concerned with the construction of a contract so as to determine the intention of the parties. That approach was not appropriate when construing a statutory provision. (2) The 1954 Act did not permit the enlargement of the holding by granting rights that had not been conferred by the expired lease.

REPAIR

We are constantly reminded that, for the purpose of lease covenants, repair generally is regarded as the restoration by renewal or replacement of subsidiary parts of the whole. Renewal, on the other hand, is reconstruction of the entirety, meaning by the entirety not necessarily the whole but substantially the whole. This follows from decided authorities.

The courts have continued, in the context both of the obligation to repair and of the impact of repairing covenants on rent review, to draw a marked contrast between repair, on the one hand, and re-building or renewal on the other. Where the covenant is genuinely one to re-build or to renew (in the sense of replacing) the landlord will be prejudiced on rent review. See, for instance, *Norwich Union* v *British Railways Board* [1987] 2 EGLR 137. In this case a discount of 27.5% was allowed against the landlord. The covenant obliged the tenant "when necessary to re-build reconstruct or replace" the demised premises over a notional term of more than 100 years.

Notwithstanding that the conventional wording of a full repairing covenant is used, the basic principle remains that the age, character and locality of the demised premises at the date of the demise will still be taken into account in judging the required standard. If the demised premises are out of repair at the commencement of the lease, a covenant to repair will be construed as requiring the tenant to put the premises into repair. The extent of the repairing covenant will be closely linked to the definition of the demised premises.

It is important to consider whether the Leasehold Property (Repairs) Act 1938 will apply to the lease and if it will, to take into account the consequences where the landlord needs to enforce the tenant's repairing covenant either by means of a damages claim or proceedings for forfeiture.

The obstacles placed in a landlord's way by the Act, particularly the need to obtain the leave of the court to proceed, can sometimes be avoided by granting the landlord a right of entry to carry out the repairs and to recover the cost as a debt from the tenant, where the tenant fails to carry them out within a specified time.

On the issue of whether this route is caught by the Act, the point has been settled by the Court of Appeal decision in *Jervis* v *Harris* [1996] 1 EGLR 78. Here it was held that the claim is, in substance, one for a debt and not one for damages. Accordingly the leave of the court was not required.

If this approach is taken the landlord should consider the following points:

- Should the power of entry be restricted to inspection for wants of repair or should it extend to breaches of other tenant covenants, e.g. alterations, decoration, window dressing, compliance with statutory requirements etc?

- The clause should not only spell out what the tenant is required to do but also when he is to start, the required standard of work and the date by which the works are to be completed.

- At what point will there be an adverse impact on rental value?

- Would such a provision now prevent the landlord from obtaining an order for specific performance of the tenant's repairing covenant?

The tenant is likely to seek some or all of the following:

- Protection against disruption of its business.
- Rights of inspection of the work.
- Bona fide estimates.
- Production of receipted accounts.
- Reversionary value impact test.
- Supervision of the works.
- Provision of warranties by third parties.

Such a right of entry should also avoid the difficulties caused for landlords by the provisions of section 18(1) of the Landlord and Tenant Act 1927 which limit the amount of the damages for breach of a repairing covenant to the amount by which the value of the landlord's reversion is diminished as a result of the breach. For instance in *Craven (Builders) Limited* v *Secretary of State for Health* [2000] 1 EGLR 126, damages of £40,000 were awarded in circumstances where the cost of repairs was assessed at £312,500. The premises in that case comprised a dilapidated listed building for which there was unlikely to be demand in the market other than from a long-term speculator who would be unlikely to bid much above unrepaired value.

It is unlikely that covenants for repair and to yield up, in their usual form will extend to the remediation of contaminated land. (The statutory regime for determining where the cost of remediation should fall is contained in Part IIA of the Environmental Protection Act 1990 which was brought into force on 1st April 2000.) Against that, covenants obliging a party to keep the premises in "good condition" may well cover such remediation, as may covenants requiring compliance with statute. Service charge provisions may also be relevant.

As a general matter, however, thought should be given to the following:

- Encouraging the parties during pre-lease negotiations to agree upon the way in which liability for land contamination should be apportioned, e.g. historic site contamination to the landlord with any addition during the term to the tenant.

- Extending conventional repairing covenants so that the remediation of contamination is expressly included, possibly by reference to some environmental baseline report akin to a schedule of condition.

- The ability of the landlord in appropriate cases to secure interim environmental schedules along the lines of interim schedules of dilapidation.

- The ability of the landlord in such cases to resort to a "self-help" clause similar to that involved in *Jervis* v *Harris* (see earlier notes).

- An environmental audit and remediation of any contamination revealed as a pre-condition to consent for assignment.

Finally, a new edition (the fourth) of the RICS Guidance Note on Dilapidations has been published. It can be purchased online at www.ricsbooks.com. Alternatively, telephone 020 7222 7000.

SERVICE CHARGES

The Code of Practice on Commercial Leases contains the following recommendation:

> *Recommendation 20: Landlords should observe the Guide to Good Practice on Service Charges in Commercial Properties. Tenants should familiarise themselves with that Guide and should take professional advice if they think that they are being asked to pay excessive service charges.*

The first edition of the Guide was produced in 1994 under the auspices of the RICS, ISVA, the British Property Federation, the British Retail Consortium and three other industry bodies. It was a very brief document that attracted little publicity or comment. A second much expanded edition was produced under similar auspices in August 2000, and was published shortly thereafter. (A number of detailed appendices on this occasion contain examples of what is considered to be good practice and illustrate how some of the principles outlined in the Guide may be achieved.) Copies of the Guide can be freely downloaded from www.servicechargeguide.co.uk .

The principal aims of the Guide, while recognising that in providing the services in a multi-occupied development the owner's objective will be to maintain the quality and value of his investment with 100% recovery of the costs incurred, would appear to be to:

1 Promote good administrative and business practice between owners and occupiers in the management of services in commercial properties.

2 Encourage good working relationships to secure co-operation between owners and occupiers through consultation and communication about what services are required, their quality and cost.

This is intended to be achieved by excellent communications and transparency in the way that services and their costs are managed and administered.

The specific topics covered by the Guide are:

1 Service charge costs

2 Value for money

3 Transparency

4 Communications

5 Promotions

6 Income

7 Management

8 Management fees

9 Apportionment

10 Budgets/accounts

11 Sinking funds

If the Government does choose to legislate, so as to give statutory force to certain of the principles set out in the Code of Practice on Commercial Leases, then there must be a distinct possibility that any such legislation will extend to service charges also, and to some of the principles set out in the Guide. (At present there is no direct legislation to consider in the commercial sector and limited impact from the common law. The terms of the lease itself are all important.) There is, of course, an existing model for new legislation to be found in the statutory regime governing service charges in residential leasehold properties.

Let us take a number of the more concrete recommendations contained in the Guide and consider their impact on the parties to a commercial lease in the event that statutory force were to be given to them. Inevitably, as with the Code, many recommendations amount to little more than an exhortation to the parties to deal with each other in an honest and transparent way. The parliamentary draftsman's first task would be to distil a set of distinct principles from the more particularly worded recommendations.

Service Charge Costs

The Guide contains three specific recommendations in relation to the extent of service charge costs, supported by seven further recommendations in relation to value for money. In essence, service charge costs are restricted to those properly incurred, including the reasonable costs of maintenance, repair and replacement of "fabric, plant, equipment and materials necessary for the property".

Enhancement costs are also envisaged in certain circumstances, and in a separate section of the Guide it is recommended that the funding of promotional activities should be shared between landlord and tenant.

There are a limited number of specific exclusions, such as initial costs relating to the design and construction of the property and costs that are a matter between the landlord and a specific tenant, e.g. those in respect of letting, rent collection, and enforcement of covenants. Elsewhere, it is made clear that service charge costs attributable to unlet units, or to elements of the property used by the landlord for his own purposes, should not be charged to the tenant.

For obvious reasons, there is no definition of the specific services to be provided, and no sweeping-up clause. (However, one of the introductory recommendations is that they should be beneficial and relevant to the needs of the landlord and the tenant and the tenant's customers.) Similarly there are no recommendations as to the level of obligation upon the landlord to provide the services or as to the circumstances in which he should be immune from liability for a failure to provide them.

(The principle of value for money is dealt with in a much less cohesive way.)

Put into statutory form, these recommendations would import both a test of good faith ("properly incurred") and a test of reasonableness ("reasonable costs"). It is very doubtful, on the basis of the decisions of the Court of Appeal in *Havenridge* v *Boston Dyers Limited* [1994] 2 EGLR 73 and *Berrycroft Management Co Limited* v *Sinclair Gardens Investments (Kensington) Limited* [1997] 1 EGLR 47, that a tenant would at present have the benefit of either in the absence of express words. This would be a distinct improvement from the point of view of tenants.

However, following on from the decisions in *Scottish Mutual Asssurance plc* v *Jardine Public Relations Limited* [1999] EGCS 43 and *Fluor Daniel Properties Limited* v *Shortlands Investments Limited* [2001] 2 EGLR 103 a tenant would these days additionally want to see express wording obliging the landlord to take into account the original length of the term of his lease, when determining whether any individual item of service charge cost was reasonable.

A tenant would also expect in most cases to see a much longer list of specific exclusions, particularly in relation to costs recoverable from insurers or other third parties, and the costs of eradicating latent or inherent defects in the property and the remediation of historic site contamination.

Most tenants would also argue that advertising and promotional costs are for the landlord to pay if they relate to the property itself. Against that, retail and leisure tenants will often recognise that they should contribute to the extent that their businesses are at the same time deriving benefit from the promotional activities in question.

Income

There are four specific recommendations in respect of income derived from services and activities in common areas. Where the service or activity is funded as a service charge cost, the income in question is to be treated as a service charge credit. Where the landlord retains income from a more established activity, such as a vending kiosk on a retail development, this should be treated as a separate letting for the purposes of apportioning service charge costs. Income receipts should be shown separately in the service charge accounts.

Given statutory form, this would satisfy most tenants. Landlords might wish to see provision made for payment of tax due on the income received.

Apportionment

These provisions are always some of the most crucial. The approach adopted in the case of any development is going to be influenced by a number of factors including the nature of the development, the identity of the landlord, whether the extent of the development is likely to vary, any mixed uses and whether rateable values have already been assessed.

The most commonly chosen methods of determining proportions involve the tenant in paying (a) a fixed amount (b) a fair proportion (c) a set percentage (d) a proportion based upon comparative rateable values (e) a proportion based upon comparative floor areas. (In this last instance particularly, a tiered approach is sometimes grafted on where specific tenants derive a lesser degree of benefit than other tenants from a specific service or facility.)

For reasons as diverse as flexibility, security, certainty and general peace of mind, most commercial leases these days will provide for the apportionment of service charge costs to be calculated according to the ratio which the floor area of the demised premises bears from time to time to the total floor area of the property. (But from the total floor area of the property, there should obviously be excluded all areas not intended for letting and used in common by all of the tenants, unless it is intended – and this is most unlikely – that the landlord should bear the proportion of the service costs relating to those common areas.)

Adoption of this method of apportionment provides flexibility in the event of the development being extended or the size of individual units changing. To avoid initial disputes, however, it is essential to specify in the leases the method of floor measurement, e.g. gross internal area, net internal area etc. Ideally, the current edition of the RICS Code of Measuring Practice should be incorporated. (From 1st December 2001 this is the fifth edition. The stated purpose of the new edition remains the same, though it takes into account new practices in measurement and includes for the first time a special use definition for leisure properties. Copies can be obtained form RICS Books – www.ricsbooks.org.) Failing that, there may well be need for provisions dealing with disputes.

(A further refinement, common in the case of retail developments, is to apply a weighted floor area formula. To achieve this, the floor area is weighted by dividing it into bands and a progressively greater discount is applied to each band. This may result in the tenants of smaller units paying proportionately more, but against that they benefit from the presence of the anchor tenant.)

The Guide recommends that apportionment should be on a fair and reasonable basis and should have regard to "the physical size, nature of use and benefit to" the tenants. There should be a published apportionment schedule (with an example provided) and the estimate of service charge costs and the annual accounts should set out the method and calculation used in arriving at the apportionment.

The provision of an apportionment schedule should at least prevent the tenant from worrying that the landlord was recovering in all more than 100% of the cost of providing the services. (This is not unheard of!)

In an ideal world – and with a responsible landlord – there are distinct advantages in simply providing for each tenant to pay a "fair and reasonable" proportion of the cost of the services. (The landlord may give some statement of intent as to the basis of calculation.) The advantage of this method is that it allows for variation if the development expands or the size of the units changes, and the landlord will be able to take into account all relevant circumstances, including actual benefit of the relevant services to each tenant.

But the objection commonly raised is that it leaves the tenant with uncertainty and provides scope for abuse. There will usually need to be incorporated into the lease some mechanism for dealing with disputes. To a certain extent this then tends to rob the provisions of its simplicity. Most tenants would not be happy with this approach.

If this is to be regulated by statute, then the more satisfactory approach is the comparative floor areas formula.

Estimates

It goes without saying that a tenant will always want to know that any estimate of likely service charge costs will be produced in good time, will be fair and reasonable and will be reliable. The service charge will usually be the largest expenditure that the tenant has to meet in respect of the demised premises, other than rent.

The Guide recommends that a landlord should produce the estimate at least one month before the commencement of the service charge year. It should provide an adequately detailed and comprehensive summary of items of expenditure in a reasonably consistent form. There should be sufficient information to enable the tenants to make a comparison with the most recently published annual service charge accounts.

This is an area in respect of which it would not be difficult to draft legislation, and the recommendations of the Guide would provide adequate safeguards for a tenant. However, a landlord would be concerned at the absence of any mechanism for the payment of periodic instalments on account.

Annual accounts

The recommendations in relation to the production of annual accounts are merged with those relating to estimates. In fact, the Guide sets out in fine detail the minimum information that the landlord should provide to the tenant with each.

In summary, the landlord should submit certified accounts to the tenants in a timely manner and in any event within six months of the year end. The tenants should be allowed a reasonable period in which to raise enquiries. The landlord should deal with any enquiries promptly and efficiently, and make relevant papers available for inspection.

The accounts should give an adequately detailed and comprehensive summary of items of expenditure, in a reasonably consistent format, with a clear correlation between a head of expenditure and its breakdown. They should be certified by an "auditor", and the cost charged as a service charge cost. (Does this mean a person qualified to audit the accounts of a registered company?) The tenant should be allowed an independent audit but at his own expense.

Again, this is an area in respect of which it would be straightforward to legislate. It is not clear whether the accounts should be prepared on an expenditure incurred as opposed to an expenditure paid basis. Whether an audit is essential is questionable, as long as the accounts are certified by an independent professional. In either case, the process is only an assurance that the sums referred to have been incurred or paid by the landlord. (This is supported by the wording of the specimen certificate provided.) It is no guarantee that the landlord has complied with the terms of the lease in providing a particular service, or that excessive expenditure is not involved.

The six-month period is probably over generous. No recommendations are made in respect of the inevitable balancing exercise, though examples of expenditure and service charge variance reports are given.

In conclusion, some may see it fanciful to anticipate statutory regulation of service charges in respect of commercial properties, and possibly before the events leading up to the publication of the present edition of the Code last year it would have been. However, there have always been tenant concerns about uncertainty, unaccountability and a lack of control and a changing market has seen landlords having to agree to caps or index-linking. There has also been a move to inclusive rents in some sectors. The present Government has criticised the commercial property industry for not providing the business sector with an appropriate level of choice. If at some stage in the future an attempt is made to legislate on service charges in commercial properties, the starting point will be the Guide.

SET-OFF

In any case where the landlord is seeking to recover arrears of rent, it is open to the tenant to claim a right of equitable set-off in respect of monies due to him from the landlord. The right of set-off operates as an abatement of the rent. The tenant's claim must arise either under the lease or under another agreement closely connected with the lease. It may be liquidated or unliquidated.

For instance, in *British Anzani (Felixstowe) Limited* v *International Marine Management (UK) Limited* [1980] QB 137 equitable set-off was allowed for £1 million in respect of the landlord's failure to repair two warehouses against rent arrears of £540,000. The repairing obligation was contained not in the lease, but in a prior agreement.

In *Muscat* v *Smith* [2003] NPC 88 the Court of Appeal went so far as to hold that the right of equitable set-off could run against the offending landlord's successor in title in respect of arrears of rent assigned to him. In that case, Mr Smith had occupied a small house for some 40 years and enjoyed the protection of the Rent Acts as a statutory tenant. His landlord at the time, Mr Walker, in response to a disrepair notice served by the local authority, employed builders in 1995 to carry out remedial works. This took 20 months and caused major disruption and inconvenience to Mr Smith. He withheld his rent.

In 1999 Mr Walker sold the freehold interest to Mr Muscat and assigned the right to arrears of rent amounting to £3860 to him. Mr Muscat sought a possession order and in those proceedings the principal issue was whether

Mr Smith enjoyed a right of equitable set-off against Mr Muscat in relation to his claim for unliquidated damages against Mr Walker, the predecessor in title of Mr Muscat. The Court of Appeal held that he did. The debt, i.e. the arrears of rent, as a chose in action vested in Mr Muscat subject to all equities available to Mr Smith against Mr Walker, his former landlord.

Obviously, where a "clear" lease is intended, the landlord will always seek to exclude the right of equitable set-off. Such an attempt was upheld by the High Court in *Electricity Supply Nominees* v *IAF Group Limited* [1993] 2 EGLR 95. Here the tenant sought to set-off damages for breach of a landlord's repairing covenant against a claim for rent. It attempted to rely upon the Unfair Contract Terms Act 1977, albeit that the Act is stated – in Schedule 1 para 1(b) – not to apply to "any contract so far as it relates to the creation or transfer of an interest in land". The tenant argued that only that part of the lease which created the interest in the land (i.e. the demise) was outside the provisions of the Act, with the result that the Act applied to the clause excluding set-off.

The court rejected this argument and held that all of the covenants which were integral to the lease that created the interest in land "related to" the creation of that interest in land. This included the covenant to pay rent. Accordingly the defence of set-off was not available to the tenant.

A similar decision was reached in *Star Rider Ltd* v *Inntrepreneur Pub Co* [1998] 1 EGLR 53 and both of these High Court decisions were subsequently held to be correct ones by the Court of Appeal in *Unchained Growth III plc* v *Granby Village (Manchester) Management Co Limited* [2000] 1 WLR 739. In that case tenants failed in their contention that service charge provisions contained in a number of residential leases (including provisions excluding the tenant's right of equitable set-off) were subject to the provisions of the 1977 Act. The court held that the provisions were an integral part of the lease, and that to conclude that they did not relate to the creation of the leasehold interest would be to lose sight of commercial reality.

For the right of set-off to be excluded, however, there will need to be explicit wording in the lease. The Court of Appeal has held that the words "without any deduction" are insufficient by themselves, in the absence of any context suggesting the contrary, to operate by implication as an exclusion of the tenant's right of equitable set-off. See the decision of the Court of Appeal in *Connaught Restaurants Limited* v *Indoor Leisure Limited* [1994] 1 WLR 501.

SHORT-TERM LEASES

There have been many attempts, over many years, to introduce standard form leases suitable for short-term lettings. For example, in 1991 the Law Society's Business Lease was introduced to some acclaim. However, it is rarely encountered today. The British Property Federation (BPF) has been more successful in encouraging the use of industry-standard documentation.

At the beginning of 1998, the BPF issued a consultation document comprising a draft agreement, draft lease, introductory statement and guidance notes. It sought comments, and support, for a form of lease with all inclusive charges, no unexpected costs or terminal claims and an ability for both parties either to walk away at the end of the day or to choose to sign up again. The draft lease was targeted at a much more limited range of letting transactions than the Law Society's Business Lease and was, therefore, likely to be rather more focused.

Perhaps more importantly, the exercise took place at a stage when the property industry had become much more accustomed to catering for the specific needs of its customers, and property lawyers had become much more aware of the benefits flowing from the preparation of even-handed documentation.

In April 1999, the agreement and lease were published, and are now available on the BPF website – www.bpf.org.uk. There is also a facility on that website which allows the documents to be completed by the insertion of the necessary details.

Plain English is used in the case of each document, except where legal uncertainty might result. Clauses are short and to the point. The agreement for lease is admirably brief and is likely to be required only where the tenant is to be given access prior to the necessary court order being obtained. (In any other circumstances, the parties are likely to proceed immediately to the grant of the lease.)

These are the salient points in relation to the agreement for lease:

- The agreed form of lease is to be attached.
- The parties are obliged to obtain the court order.
- Completion of the lease is tied to the making of the order.
- Either party may rescind if the order is not obtained by a stated date.
- The tenant is allowed access, as licensee, in consideration of a rent- equivalent fee.
- Access is allowed for a maximum period of six weeks but the period ends on the earlier of completion or termination of the agreement.
- Payment on account of that fee and the rent deposit is a pre-condition.
- The benefit of the agreement is not assignable by the tenant.

(This structure does cause some slight concern. It might be argued that where an express obligation is imposed on the tenant to join in the application to the court, section 38(1) of the Landlord and Tenant Act 1954 renders the provision in question void. Furthermore, if the facts show that the tenant does have exclusive possession during this intermediate stage, the arrangement could be construed as an immediate tenancy. Often it will be preferable to substitute a tenancy at will or a short fixed term tenancy.)

To turn to the lease:

- The rent is fixed for the period of the letting and is exclusive of VAT.
- The rent is also inclusive of the cost of services, with an option for it to be inclusive of business rates also.
- As there is no obligation on the landlord to insure, by implication the rent additionally is inclusive of the cost of any insurance of the buildings maintained by the landlord.
- Payment can be required by standing order and set-off is excluded.
- There is a simple rent deposit provision, which could leave the tenant vulnerable in the event of the landlord's insolvency.
- Equally, the landlord is vulnerable in that if there is premature determination, he has no ability to cover the cost of a void.
- There is no provision for a surety to be joined.
- Charges for water, gas, electricity and telephone services are the responsibility of the tenant.
- There is an optional restricted hours provision.
- There are absolute restrictions imposed on the tenant in the case of alterations, use and alienation (other than group sharing).

- There is no obligation on the tenant to repair; merely an agreement to take reasonable care of the premises, subject to fair wear and tear, and not to damage them.

- The landlord's obligations are restricted to the equivalent of a covenant for quiet enjoyment and a reasonable endeavours undertaking in respect of stated services.

- One of the services is keeping the premises in "tenantable condition".

- The usual general provisions appear.

- There is an optional (and unconditional) break clause.

- There is also an exclusion agreement.

The BPF had it in mind that the documents would be used primarily for lettings for a few months up to one or two years. Invariably, it will not be necessary for the lease to be executed in the form of a deed in such a case. The lease is capable of being used for whole or part buildings of all kinds and for units on an estate. Both documents envisage a contracting out of the 1954 Act, though equally advantage might be taken in the appropriate circumstances of section 43(3). (This possibly should be made more obvious to users.)

A landlord will need to be confident of the overall costs of running the premises, including their repair, given that the rent is a fully inclusive one. For the same reason, he will shoulder the related risks. But in return he will be able to offer the attraction of an all-inclusive deal.

Perhaps these are the lessons to be learned from this and similar initiatives:

- That standard form documents will work in the appropriate circumstances.

- That plain English can be used safely.
- That the use of standard forms does not mean that we doubt our own drafting ability.
- That straightforward documentation can safely be prepared by less qualified fee-earners using this system.
- That low value work often does not justify individual drafting.

SINKING FUNDS

The terms "sinking fund" and "reserve fund" are not usually seen as synonymous. The purpose of a sinking fund is generally regarded as being to provide for expenditure which may occur no more than once or twice during the lifetime of a lengthy lease on specific items such as lifts, central heating boilers, air conditioning plant and roofs. In that sense it is essentially a *replacement* fund. A reserve fund, on the other hand, tends to be established to meet recurring expenditure, such as external decoration costs, in such a way that fluctuations in the annual amounts of service charge are avoided. It is essentially an *equalisation* fund.

There are some very obvious advantages in the case of sinking or replacement funds. The landlord will have funds available before incurring major expenditure and the tenant will not be faced with a disproportionately high bill in any one year.

Against that, of course, there are some equally obvious disadvantages. The tax treatment may be adverse, management and administration can be complex, and unless the fund is held on trust the tenant may become an unsecured creditor of an insolvent landlord. Furthermore, the tenant may be required to contribute to future expenditure from which he will derive no benefit if the lease expires before the work is carried out.

It is this final issue which frequently concerns tenants most, and which may involve a trap for them. See, for instance, *Secretary of State for the Environment* v *Possfund (North West) Limited* [1997] 2 EGLR 179. In that case, the tenant had paid sums into a replacement fund earmarked for the air-conditioning plant serving the premises that had been installed in 1973. (At the date of the hearing, the fund was worth around £1 million.) On the expiry of the lease in 1994, the fund had not been spent. The tenant claimed that he was entitled to recover the money. The landlord claimed the money as his own absolute property.

The court found for the landlord. It was irrelevant that the landlord had not spent the sums. The payments had *not* been made on account of future expenditure. Their true nature was that they were made to indemnify the landlord against the cost incurred by him each year by virtue of depreciation of the plant. They were, in effect, a depreciation allowance. This was also emphasised by the absence in the lease of any mechanism for repayment.

If a tenant is to avoid this approach, the lease will need to make it clear that payments into the sinking fund are made, not as a depreciation allowance but for the express purpose of funding replacement of the items in question. To the extent that such sums have not been so expended by the expiry of the lease, they are to be regarded as held upon a resulting trust for the tenant. In other words, the lease must provide a machinery for repayment.

(A landlord is better advised to retain an option to establish a sinking fund rather than actually covenanting to do so.)

If a fund is to be established, the tenant will want to know that:

- The fund is held in a separate designated account.
- The purposes for which the fund can be used are clearly stated in the lease.
- Contributions have been appropriately calculated against reliable estimates.

- The fund will be properly invested and income will accrue to it.
- Contributions cannot be used in respect of expenditure likely to be incurred after the expiry of his lease.
- The fund is held on an express trust with the tenants for the time being identified as beneficiaries.

On the whole, it is frequently more beneficial for the replacement of major items to be funded by a structured borrowing programme or by means of depreciation charges. (The latter have few of the complications of sinking funds.) In fact in the *Possfund* case, what appeared on the face of it to have been accumulated as a sinking or replacement fund was found, on a true construction of the lease, to be a depreciation charge or allowance.

STATUTORY IMPROVEMENTS

As we have seen, it is generally accepted commercially that if a tenant carries out entirely voluntary improvements, with consent, to the demised premises during the term of the lease and funds the works himself, he should not be penalised on rent review. To allow the landlord to enjoy the rental uplift attributable to those improvements would be to provide him with a windfall. Protection is given to the tenant by including in the rent review provisions a fairly conventionally worded disregard. Nevertheless, attention has to be given to the drafting of the disregard, if problems are to be avoided on both sides.

For instance, it may be necessary to define in the lease what is meant by the term "improvement". (By analogy with cases on section 19(2) of the Landlord and Tenant Act 1927, the term may otherwise be construed to mean works of alteration that improve the premises from the point of view of the tenant.) Ideally, what should be the subject of the disregard is not the improvement itself but rather its effect upon rent or any increase in rental value attributable to it.

A landlord will argue that qualifying improvements should be limited to those carried out during the contractual term of the lease by the tenant or a sub-tenant. A landlord may also seek to insist upon a "rolling period" provision to deal with stale improvements. Necessary consents under the lease and any superior lease must have been obtained, and works carried out pursuant to an obligation owed to the landlord must fall outside the disregard.

What specific issues should concern a tenant? Consents under the lease may be unreasonably withheld and the benefit of the disregard lost. Pre-term improvements will need to be dealt with expressly. While the courts will be reluctant to construe a licence to alter as imposing an obligation to do the works, it may be open to a landlord – where the works are governed by an absolute covenant against alterations – to deny the tenant the benefit of the disregard. See *Daejan Properties Limited* v *Holmes* [1996] EGCS 185.

But perhaps the most serious problems for the tenant come about where the improvements are carried out pursuant to obligations in the lease that require compliance with statutes or with directions of local or other public authorities.

In *Forte & Co Limited* v *General Accident Life Assurance Limited* [1986] 2 EGLR 115, it had been necessary for the tenant to carry out works to the demised premises pursuant to the Fire Precautions Act 1971 to obtain a fire certificate. Undoubtedly, those works must have resulted in an increase in rental value. It was held, however, that the works fell outside the terms of the relevant disregard in the rent review clause because they were carried out by the tenant pursuant to an obligation owed to the landlord. The lease contained the usual covenant by the tenant with the landlord to comply with requirements of statutes and of statutory authorities.

This is a problem that can be dealt with at the lease negotiation stage by appropriate amendments to the relevant disregard.

STEPPED RENT AGREEMENTS

A landlord may well be inclined, in recessionary times, to compromise a rent review with a tenant facing financial difficulty rather than seek to conclude the review strictly in accordance with the terms of the lease and some months later have an insolvent tenant. A common form of compromise is the "stepped rent agreement" whereby the landlord agrees with the tenant to accept £x for the first two years of the forthcoming review period and £y for the remaining three years. In all likelihood £x will be less than the open market rent at the relevant review date and £y will be more.

On the face of it, such a compromise must amount to a variation of the terms of the lease. While it will not be sufficient to result in a deemed surrender and re-grant, the issue of third party liability and a possible release arises. Any current guarantor will automatically be released from future liability under his contract of guarantee, unless he is joined as a party to the stepped rent agreement and covenants to be bound by it. A landlord will, however, have in mind others who have a similar liability to him. In the case of an old tenancy, this will include former tenants and their guarantors where privity of contract still applies. In the case of a new tenancy, it will mean a former tenant who retains liability either as a result of executing an excluded assignment, or of entering into an AGA.

In *Friends' Provident Life Office* v *British Railways Board* [1995] 2 EGLR 55, the Court of Appeal overturned earlier authorities that had ruled that a former tenant was automatically bound by post-assignment variations to a lease, albeit that he was not a party to them. The result of this decision, therefore, is that obligations accepted by a former tenant as part of his original contract with his landlord cannot be varied or increased so as to bind him by a subsequent agreement entered into by the landlord with an assignee, where the former tenant is not a party to that agreement. He is not discharged from liability; he simply remains bound to the extent of his original covenants.

Ironically, Parliament was at the same time working along the same lines in enacting section 18 of the Landlord and Tenant (Covenants) Act 1995. This enacts a similar principle. The distinction, of course, is that the effect of the Court of Appeal's decision in 1995 is retrospective, whereas the statutory provision catches only variations made on or after 1st January 1996.

For that reason, section 18 was inapplicable in *Beegas Nominees Limited* v *BHP Petroleum Limited* [1998] 2 EGLR 57, a case in which the Court of Appeal further developed the *Friends' Provident* principle in the context of rent reviews. A 1981 lease for a term of 25 years had been assigned twice. The 1991 rent review was settled between the landlord and the second assignee on the basis of a stepped rent agreement. Neither the original tenant nor the first assignee was a party. Furthermore, the agreement was something that the lease did not envisage. In 1996, the second assignee went into liquidation and the lease was disclaimed.

It was held, hardly surprisingly, that the stepped rent agreement bound neither the original tenant nor the first assignee. But nor did it operate as a release. The 1991 rent review provisions continued to bind both, and the landlord was entitled to have those provisions implemented retrospectively so as to ascertain the amount of their liability for rent.

What practical lessons are there to be learnt in relation to stepped rent agreements? In practice it is most unlikely that any former tenant would volunteer to be bound by a stepped rent agreement. At best, the landlord might be able to "re-visit" the rent review, as in the present case, provided that nothing in the rent review provisions imposes a time limit for implementation. The practical difficulties are, however, obvious.

In the case of an existing lease, the landlord should be advised to initiate and conclude the rent review in strict accordance with the terms of the lease. This will then produce a single rent that will be binding also upon former tenants. Subsequently it would be open to him to agree a stepped rent arrangement with the current tenant, as a personal concession only and not as a variation of the lease terms. In the case of future leases, we have already started to see rent review provisions drafted so as to give the landlord an option to agree a stepped rent.

SUBJECT TO LICENCE

A responsible landlord of business premises appreciates the need for his tenant to have some early indication of that landlord's likely views in respect of any application made for the grant of consent under the terms of the lease. Great care must now be taken in all instances as to the manner of communication. Two particular cases demonstrate the ease with which consent may inadvertently be granted in correspondence.

In *Prudential Assurance Co Limited* v *Mount Eden Land Limited* [1997] 1 EGLR 37 the leases under which the demised premises were held provided that certain alterations could not be carried out without the landlord's "previous written consent". The leases gave that expression a very wide meaning. Consent was applied for and at one stage the landlord's agent wrote to the tenant stating as follows. "I can confirm that the freeholder... gives consent for the works, subject to the following conditions." One of the stated conditions required the tenant to enter into a formal licence. The letter itself was headed with the rubric "subject to licence". However, no formal licence was ever granted. Section 146 notices were later served alleging breaches of the alterations covenants.

The Court of Appeal held that in the context of the leases, the letter was perfectly capable, on its wording, of constituting an immediate grant of consent for the alterations in question and that it was not deprived of legal effect by the addition of the rubric "subject to licence". Where negotiations were being carried on between strangers in law, i.e. where no contractual relationship yet existed between them, it was clear that rubrics such as "subject to contract" and "subject to lease" prevented any legal liability arising. But where the parties were already legally bound, and what was contemplated was the unilateral act of one or the other – such as the grant of consent – no similar principle applied. All that was required was the act itself.

This decision was followed shortly afterwards by the High Court in *Next plc* v *National Farmers Union Mutual Insurance Co Limited* [1997] EGCS 181 in the case of an application for a licence to assign. It was held that certain letters headed "subject to licence" amounted to an immediate and binding consent. That expression had no suspensive effect in this context, and the terms of the correspondence indicated that the landlord's consent to the assignment had been given.

(For an even more recent decision of the Court of Appeal, see *Aubergine Enterprises Limited* v *Lakewood International Limited* [2002] EWCA Civ 177. Here it was held that a letter referring to "consent in principle" and headed "subject to licence" constituted formal and valid consent.)

The problem for landlords is overcome in the case of leases that stipulate adequately that any landlord's consent for the purposes of the lease must be embodied in an instrument executed as a deed by the landlord. As far as other leases are concerned, it should be made clear in the initial correspondence that the landlord has no intention whatsoever of granting any consent unless and until it is embodied in an instrument executed as a deed by the landlord. A landlord is further protected by the avoidance of phrases or expressions that might be construed as an indication of immediate consent. It is also open to the writer of the letter to incorporate a denial of agency.

SURRENDERS

As we have seen, surrender is a consensual act that results in the determination of the term of the lease. It may follow an agreement for surrender, but where the lease comprises a business tenancy within the Landlord and Tenant Act 1954, the agreement will presently be void unless authorised by the court under section 38(4) of the Act.

A surrender of part may take place. It operates as such and should not imply the grant of a new lease of the remainder, though its effect may be to release an existing guarantor from future liability. A sub-lease survives the surrender of the head lease even where the sub-lease had been granted in breach of covenant. Where a surrender and re-grant occurs, existing sub-leases are preserved.

A surrender also operates to release the present parties to the lease from future liability, but not liability for past breaches of covenant. Former tenants and guarantors are similarly released. A properly advised tenant will always therefore seek to negotiate in addition an express release in respect of liability that has accrued at the date of the surrender.

Does any particular problem arise for landlords in the context of surrenders? There is a difficulty when it comes to what are sometimes known as "dying breath" obligations in the lease which is to be surrendered. These are obligations that are stated to arise "at the expiration or on the sooner determination" of the lease. Typically they relate to the state and condition of the premises.

Assume a lease that contains such an obligation to re-decorate the interior of the demised premises. The landlord's original intention in relation to the imposition of the covenant may well have been to ensure that on lease expiry, the premises would be yielded up in sufficient internal decorative repair to enable them to be marketed immediately. A surrender is negotiated mid-term. Will the landlord be able to enforce that obligation given that the surrender will amount to "the sooner determination" of the lease.

It would seem that in the absence of a freshly imposed obligation within the deed of surrender, he will not. In *Re ABC Coupler and Engineering Co Limited (No 3)* [1970] 1 All ER 650, the High Court held that an obligation in a surrendered lease to yield up the premises with full vacant possession "at the expiration or sooner determination of the said term" did not survive the surrender of the lease. Any breach could not be regarded as antecedent to the surrender. Where such obligations are to be preserved, therefore, unless they are to be translated into payment of an agreed sum of money as a condition of the surrender, they will need to be re-imposed in the deed of surrender itself.

TERM OF LEASE

The expression "term commencement date" appears frequently in interpretation clauses in leases as a specified date. More often than not, the date will coincide with the most recently expired quarter day at the date of grant of the lease. Premises will then typically be demised to the tenant "to hold the same for a term of *x* years from and including the term commencement date".

It would, however, be more accurate to use an alternative expression such as "term calculation date" since what we are inevitably referring to is the date from which the length of the term is computed. This is because, as a matter of strict law, the earliest date from which the term of a lease may commence is the date of completion of the grant of the lease itself. Obviously a lease may be granted for a term commencing on some future date, but such a lease will be rendered void by section 149(3) of the Law of Property Act 1925 if that date is more than 21 years after the date of the lease.

Where a lease is silent as to the date on which the term is to commence, it follows that the court will assume the parties to have intended it to commence on the date of the lease itself. Does any of this really cause a problem in practice? Probably not, but difficulties can arise when the term of a lease is stated to commence "from" a particular date.

The basic rule is that the date is then *excluded* from the term with the result that the term expires contractually on the anniversary date. But ambiguity can arise. Whether the word "from" should be construed in this way depends ultimately on the context. The basic rule will be displaced, for instance, where it is clear from the lease that the parties intended rent to be paid in respect of that named day, or where the term of an earlier lease between the same parties came to an end on the previous day. In those circumstances, the named day will be *included*.

One importance of knowing exactly when the term expires contractually is that it will govern the validity of notices served under section 25 and requests made under section 26 of the Landlord and Tenant Act 1954. In *Whelton Sinclair* v *Hyland* [1992] 2 EGLR 158 the lease had been granted for a term of ten years "from 27th June 1976". A section 25 notice had been served on the tenant purporting to terminate the tenancy on 26th June 1986. The tenant contended that the notice was invalid. The contractual term did not expire until 27th June 1986. The Court of Appeal upheld the validity of the notice, finding that the basic rule was displaced for the reasons referred to above.

The problem again is avoided in the context of this Act if the date chosen as the termination date in the notice, or the date for commencement of the new tenancy in the request, is a date some days beyond the ultimate date on which it might be argued that the term has expired contractually.

THIRD PARTY DETERMINATION

The basic distinction between an expert and an arbitrator is one of function. The job of the arbitrator is to resolve a settled dispute by reference to evidence and submissions put to him by the parties. His award must be made on the basis of that evidence. The role of an expert is to answer a specific question by reference to his own knowledge and experience, e.g. on rent review, what is the amount of the new rent. He acts upon his own skill and judgment. (It must be accepted, however, that the powers given to an arbitrator by the Arbitration Act 1996 tend now to blur the basic distinction somewhat.) What are the specific duties and attributes of each?

Arbitrator

- He is immune from actions in negligence.
- In principle he must act "judicially" and, in particular must hear both sides and must reach his decision on the evidence, not on the basis of his own expertise.
- He can compel disclosure of evidence and attendance of witnesses.
- He can order payment of fees and his own fees may be taxed by the court.
- His award is enforceable as a judgment of the court.
- The procedures of an arbitration, including appeals are governed by statute.

- There is a right of appeal to the court against his award on a point of law.

Expert

- He *may* be liable for negligence.
- He is free to reach a decision based on his own expertise and can thus arrive at a figure outside the parameters of those of the parties. This has the important consequence that his figure does not have to be based on admissible evidence.
- He is free to adopt whatever procedures he chooses (except insofar as the terms of his appointment lay down a procedure).
- He does not have the same procedural powers as an arbitrator; notably, he has no inherent power to order the payment of costs (although he may be given a contractual power to do so).
- His determination cannot be enforced as such.
- His fees cannot be taxed.
- No legislation governs the exercise of his functions.
- There is limited ability to challenge his decision on a point of law.

In the context of rent review disputes, the following general perceptions may also affect the choice:

- In theory at least, expert determination is quick and cheap and allows an agency view to be taken.
- With expert determination, there is an emphasis on finality but reasoned decisions are rarely given.

- Expert determination is ideal where the property is of a common type and specification and comparables are likely to abound.

- Arbitration tends to be slower and more expensive but reasoned awards must now be given, unless the parties agree otherwise.

- The Arbitration Act 1996 allows the parties a great deal of freedom in terms of deciding how the arbitration should be conducted.

- Arbitration allows an opportunity for cross-examination of the other side's expert witness and for full argument.

- Arbitration is more suitable where points of law are likely to arise, and where there are few comparables.

For an example of the present approach of the court to the role of a rent review arbitrator see *Checkpoint Limited* v *Strathclyde Pension Fund* [2003] EWHC 439. The lease in question provided that if on rent review the parties could not agree the amount of the revised rent, it was to be determined by " a chartered surveyor experienced in the letting and/or valuation of property that is of a similar nature to the premises and is situated in the same region as the premises and used for purposes similar to those authorised under this lease". The parties failed to agree the amount of the revised rent on the first review due under the lease, and an arbitrator was appointed. He confirmed to the parties that if he used his inquisitorial powers, he would inform them of his findings and ask them to comment.

In determining the new rent, the arbitrator accepted the comparables put forward on behalf of the landlord, basing his decision – in part – on his own experience of lettings in the locality where those comparables were situated. The tenant appealed to the High Court challenging the arbitrator's award on the ground of serious irregularity. Its main contention was that the arbitrator had not been entitled to rely upon his own experience, in particular, upon matters for which he had been given no evidence. The appeal was dismissed. The tenant then appealed to the Court of Appeal.

The Court of Appeal dismissed the appeal. The appeal judges said that a line had to be drawn between the use of general knowledge, and the use of specialised knowledge. It was the latter that was proscribed. In this case, the arbitrator was simply using the range of knowledge that the terms of the lease anticipated that he would have. He had acted fairly. He was using that knowledge for the purpose of evaluating the evidence before him, rather than setting out fresh evidence on a point that had previously not been raised. Furthermore, he had not exercised his inquisitorial powers, nor had he made independent enquiries of anyone.

It should be borne in mind that section 34 of the Arbitration Act 1996 gave arbitrators for the first time the power to adopt an inquisitorial approach to evidential matters, and so to that extent one of the main distinctions between the role of an arbitrator and that of an expert has become blurred. The main issue in this case, however, was a separate one namely whether the arbitrator had used his own expert knowledge as evidence without putting that evidence to the parties. Had he done so, the court would have been entitled to ask itself whether this amounted to a serious irregularity for the purposes of section 68 of the Act. If there is shown to be a serious irregularity, the court may remit the award for reconsideration, set the award aside or declare it to be of no effect.

TURNOVER RENTS

Here the success of the tenant's business governs, usually in part only, the amount of the rent that he pays. (They are popular with tenants, therefore, in recessionary times.) To work effectively, they require a greater than usual degree of co-operation from landlords, and a willingness on the part of tenants to disclose business information that they would not normally expect to.

In the case of retail or quasi-retail premises, success is usually measured in terms of turnover. Typically in shopping centres, a base rent of, say, 80% of the unit's open market rental will be payable together with a percentage of the tenant's turnover. Sometimes now this turnover element can be assessed and levied electronically at the end of each day's trading. Petrol stations, hotels, pubs and restaurants are also let on a similar basis from time to time. Difficulties may abound, however, depending upon the nature of the business in question and the detailed method of its operation by the tenant.

For instance, a problem arises for retail landlords where the tenant's business involves internet sales. The premises may well in effect have become a showroom to prompt on-line sales via the internet. Appropriate provisions can be inserted in leases but there will often be practical difficulties in enforcing them. Perhaps the safest course here for a landlord is to reserve the option to switch to open market rent in given circumstances. (They might also include a proposed assignment.)

These are some general points to bear in mind:

- Exactly what should be included within turnover? (The tenant's expenditure is not relevant but common deductions are VAT, staff discounts, trade-in allowances and cash refunds for defective goods sold from the premises.)
- How are in-store concessions to be dealt with?
- Should any basic rent be subject to conventional review?
- Should a maximum turnover be set?
- Where discounts are commonly given, should the full retail price be brought into account?
- Should there be provision for bad debts?
- Should the landlord have a power to inspect the tenant's books following audit?
- Should there be independent determination of turnover in the case of dispute?
- Should a positive trading covenant be inserted in the lease?
- Should there be an absolute restriction on franchising arrangements and subletting etc. of part?
- What controls on assignment should be imposed to ensure the appropriate tenant mix?
- Should the landlord insist upon the lease being contracted out with an obligation to offer back as a pre-condition to assignment?
- Any related keep-open clause should provide for payment of liquidated damages in the event of breach.

It will be interesting to see whether acceptance of the Code of Practice on Commercial Leases results in an increase in rental arrangements tied to turnover or performance. The potential for annual growth might in some cases compensate for the loss of upward only rent reviews.

UNDERLETTING

Problems can occur where a lease imposes a requirement that any underlease granted out of it must reserve a specific level of rent. This is illustrated by the decision of the Court of Appeal in *Allied Dunbar Assurance plc* v *Homebase Limited* [2002] 2 EGLR 23.

In that case Homebase occupied a retail unit under a 25-year lease with five yearly upward only rent reviews expiring in 2010. Allied Dunbar was the landlord. At the relevant time (June 2000) the passing rent was £322,500. In a difficult market for such a unit, Homebase, wishing to close down, had finally been able to negotiate heads of terms with Lairdale for an underlease of the whole for the unexpired residue of the term of the lease. Those heads of terms envisaged an initial rent of only £200,000, rising to £322,500 on the remaining rent review date.

The lease contained a qualified covenant against underletting. That covenant was subject to the following provisos, namely that any underlease would (1) not reserve a rent less than the then full market rent (2) contain the same covenants as the lease, and (3) provide for upward only rent reviews on the same dates as the lease did.

Homebase submitted to Allied Dunbar in support of its application to underlet a draft underlease purporting to reserve a rent of £322,500 and appearing to comply with the requirements of provisos (2) and (3). It also submitted a draft collateral deed in favour of Lairdale which contained an undertaking (*inter alia*) to pay Lairdale the difference between the rent referred to in the heads of terms and that payable under the proposed underlease. It also contained an indemnity in respect of the cost of repairs to the floor of the unit.

Allied Dunbar applied to the High Court for an order restraining Homebase from underletting the unit to Lairdale. Homebase counter-claimed for damages under the Landlord and Tenant Act 1988 for an unreasonable refusal of consent to underlet. Bernard Livesey QC, sitting as a deputy judge, found for Allied Dunbar. These are the specific points to note from the his judgment reported at [2002] L & TR 1:

- In the light of *Bocardo SA* v *S & M Hotels Limited* [1979] 2 EGLR 48, it is clear that each of the three provisos had to be complied with before the issue of reasonableness had to be considered. In other words, they were pre-conditions to the application.

- The burden of proof in that respect lay with Homebase, in contrast to the rules laid down by the Landlord and Tenant Act 1988 on refusal of consent.

- The underlease and the collateral deed had to be read together because they were "interdependent" in the sense laid down in *AG Securities Limited* v *Vaughan* [1988] 2 EGLR 78, i.e. they would both have been signed or neither.

- As a consequence of this, the underlease rent had to be viewed as £200,000 but, as a fact, such a rent could not be regarded as less than full market rent given the difficulties that Homebase had encountered in trying to find an undertenant for the unit. The first proviso had been complied with.

- The second proviso (repeating the material terms of the lease) had also been complied with.

- However, it could not be said that the third proviso had been complied with because the provision in the collateral deed for a fixed rent to be payable throughout the term of the underlease was inconsistent with the intention that the underlease should be subject to aligned upwards only rent reviews.

Homebase appealed to the Court of Appeal.

The Court of Appeal dismissed the appeal, upholding the reasoning of the deputy judge, though disagreeing with his conclusion that the second proviso had been met. (The overall consequence of the underletting agreement was that Lairdale was to effect repairs partly at its own expense and partly at the expense of Homebase.)

Furthermore, it made no difference that the collateral deed was expressed to be personal to Homebase and Lairdale. Allied Dunbar had a commercial interest in the terms of the underlease. The rent payable under it would be relevant on a review of the headlease rent. On a renewal under Part II of the Landlord and Tenant Act 1954 the terms of the underletting agreement could subsequently become the terms of the new tenancy between Allied Dunbar and Lairdale.

(The landlord would also be at a disadvantage when serving a notice under section 6 of the Law of Distress Amendment Act 1908, requiring the undertenant to pay rent directly to him.)

Permission to Homebase to appeal was refused by the House of Lords. The ruling by the Court of Appeal stands, therefore, and suggests that it will always be impossible to circumvent the terms of the headlease by resorting to a separate deed.

Are any other tactics available where a tenant seeks to offload surplus space but faces a requirement in the lease that underlettings must be at the equivalent of market rent – or even some higher passing rent – and the present review pattern incorporated in the underlease? It will depend on how dire the circumstances of the tenant are, but the options available will rarely be acceptable to a properly advised undertenant.

The tenant might ask the landlord to waive his rights under the alienation clause. The landlord will inevitably have an absolute discretion in that respect and it is difficult to imagine circumstances where there would be a any real incentive for a landlord to do this without there being some *quid pro quo* available. It also alerts the landlord to the tenant's difficulty.

The tenant might be inclined to apply for consent to underlet without revealing the arrangements entered into with the proposed undertenant. (This could, separately, involve difficult professional issues for the solicitors acting for the tenant.) Any consent granted by the landlord in such circumstances would be liable to be set aside on the landlord applying to the court, with the result that the underletting would become an unlawful one. This would hardly appeal to the undertenant.

The tenant might equally be inclined to proceed to underlet without consent. This would produce an underlease that was immediately unlawful. Again, few undertenants would be happy with this.

In either case, the landlord could take steps to forfeit the headlease but with the equally available remedies of injunctive relief and a damages claim to fall back on where the premises were likely to prove difficult to re-let at the passing rent.

USE

A tenant should always be conscious that there is no implied covenant or warranty by the landlord that the demised premises are legally or physically fit for any purpose. It is down to the tenant to seek professional advice as to the physical state and condition of the premises, to verify that any necessary planning permissions subsist and that there are no restrictions affecting the landlord's title that would prevent his intended use of the premises.

A common reaction on the part of a commercial landlord, faced with an application from his tenant for a licence to change the use of the premises, is probably to look for some payment from him. This is, of course, feasible where the covenant against change of use is in absolute terms but such covenants tend to come back and haunt landlords on rent review. More often than not the covenant will be in qualified form, which means that the landlord is faced with the provisions of section 19(3) of the 1927 Act.

Those provisions imply into qualified covenants against change of use a proviso that "no fine or sum of money in the nature of a fine, whether by way of increase of rent or otherwise, shall be payable for" the landlord's licence in any case where the proposed change of use does not involve structural alterations to the demised premises.

(The landlord will still be able to require payment of costs in connection with the grant of consent and a reasonable sum in respect of any damage to or diminution in value of the demised premises or any neighbouring property belonging to him.)

Is there a way around this problem for a landlord? Probably not, without the landlord encountering difficulties of another kind. This is clearly illustrated by the decision of the High Court in *Barclays Bank plc* v *Daejan Investments (Grove Hall) Limited* [1995] 1 EGLR 68. The tenant held premises under two long leases that restricted the use of the premises to use for banking purposes and "for no other purposes whatsoever without the consent of the landlords first obtained".

The tenant applied for a licence to change the use of the ground floor of the demised premises to uses within Class A (2) of the Town and Country Planning (Use Classes) Order 1987. Certain alterations to an exterior wall of the demised premises were to be involved in this connection. The landlord indicated by letter that a licence would be granted but only upon terms. One of the terms stipulated for was the insertion of break rights in the landlord's favour into the leases. The tenant objected.

The judge ultimately found, on the evidence, that the proposed alterations were structural ones. Section 19(3) did not therefore apply. Nevertheless, for the purpose of his judgment he considered what the position would have been had there been no structural alterations involved with the result that section 19(3) did apply.

He held that the requirement for landlord's break rights amounted to a demand for a fine because the option to break was unlikely to be exercised unless there was some financial advantage to the landlord at the time. On the basis of the decision of the Court of Appeal in *West* v *Gwynne* [1911] 2 Ch 1, the refusal to grant consent without payment of a fine would have relieved the tenant from the obligation to obtain consent for that specific change of use. The tenant would have been entitled to a declaration that the ground floor premises could be used for any Class A (2) use.

There are two lessons to learn. The first is that the court is likely interpret "fine" for this purpose as meaning any benefit on which a monetary value can be placed. It must therefore be very difficult to disguise a fine. The second is that a refusal to grant consent without payment of a fine may hand the change of use to the tenant on a plate.

Finally, In the case of user covenants, the provisions of the Landlord and Tenant Act 1988 do not apply. Tenants are sometimes inclined to forget that, in the absence of express wording in the lease, even where the covenant is fully qualified:

- There is no duty upon the landlord to respond to the application within a reasonable time.
- There is no obligation on the landlord to give reasons for a refusal or for the imposition of conditions.
- There is no duty on the landlord not unreasonably to withhold consent with the result that a claim in damages will not be available to the tenant.

For an illustration of the difficulties a tenant may face, see *London & Argyll Developments Limited* v *Mount Cook Land Limited* [2003] PLSCS 131. In that case, the landlord owned a number of properties in a mixed-use area, including the subject premises, which had previously been used as the University of Westminster student union building. The tenant sought consent to apply for planning permission and for a change of use to Class D1 (non-residential institutions). In both cases the lease provided that the landlord's consent could not be unreasonably withheld. The landlord refused consent on the grounds that an influx of students into the area would compromise its other business interests, and that – as they were situated in an established office location – the premises were best suited to development as offices. The tenant sought a declaration that the landlord's consent had been unreasonably withheld.

Lloyd J granted the declaration. The landlord's first argument was unfounded. Class D1 provided substantial scope for educational use at a range of levels. The landlord had made no attempt to ascertain the type of use or to negotiate with the tenant. Its refusal was "not only unreasonable but unreasoned". He ordered the landlord to pay indemnity costs.

INDEX

[all references are to page number]

property publishing from emis professional publishing

emis property service

emis's new property service is a unique combination of updating and practical articles presented in a new and exciting combination of media. Together it will keep you up to date with a minimum of effort, and provide an archive of practical "how-to" articles that will help solve your client's problems.

The EMIS Property Service

Incorporating Marplus

Editors:

John Martin LLB (London), LLM (Michigan), Solicitor, Director of Property Law Research, Pinsent Curtis

Professor Peter Reekie, solicitor and lecturer

Brian Kilcoyne BA (Oxon) Law, Solicitor, Lewis Silkin

Desmond Kilcoyne LLB (Southampton), LLM (London – Commercial Law), Barrister, Arden Chambers

Guy Williams, Barrister, 2 Mitre Court Buildings

Qdos Consulting

Property practitioners need incisive, interpretative information that gets to the heart of law and practice.

This new service combines the virtues of several existing services into a new wider service in:

- 12 paper issues per year
- 12 email issues per year
- A fully searchable archive in Seneca EP
- Columns on all aspects of property
- Regular updates on case and legislative developments.

Subscribers receive both "how-to" articles and updating materials across the whole range of contentious and non-contentious aspects of property.

Contents include:

- Real property
- Commercial property
- Residential property
- Agriculture
- Planning
- Domestic landlord and tenant
- VAT on Property

Articles will be presented as checklists, notes for guidance on difficult issues, diagrams, points to watch and other formats appropriate to the topic.

Updates will be sent to a designated email address in the first week of every month – which can include any number of email addresses within the subscribing firm.

The Seneca EP electronic service provides a single user licence free within the service to allow the whole archive to be searched at the same time. Your own articles and notes can be added to the records. A network version can be purchased which will allow the firm to share information within the property department.

Pages: 16, A4 Newsletter (12 per annum) 12 e-mail bulletins per annum and single user licence for electronic service

Price: £210 per annum

For a free sample, simply ring Rob Owen on 01707 334823 and let us know your postal and email address.

Rights of Way

Simon Blackford, Barrister

Rights of access to land have never been more topical. The Government's Rights to Roam proposals mean that landowners and ramblers alike must look afresh at the issue. Solicitors must offer accurate advice at a time of change. Local government, caught in the middle, must play a difficult hand – advising neutrally in an area likely to stoke passions. Simon Blackford's guide is succinctly written, providing a guide that will be invaluable to all these constituencies.

£24.00 1999 ISBN: 1 85811 166 8

Commercial Leases: 50 Traps for the Unwary

John Martin, LLB (London), LLM (Michigan), Solicitor, Director of Property Law Research, Pinsent Curtis

This unique text brings together, fully referenced and indexed, John Martin's popular short pieces for advisers of landlords and tenants in commercial leases. Written in a clear and authoritative style, the book is laid out in a tried and tested format designed to maximise the usefulness to the practitioner when faced with a particular "Trap". Faced with issues such as a Split Reversion, a "Hybrid" Tenancy or an Either Way Review, potential traps are highlighted, clarified and can be avoided in straightforward fashion. Individuals, solicitors, surveyors, local authority officers and all others involved in the construction or management of property will find the work invaluable.

£38.00 1999 ISBN 185811 218 4

Contaminated Land: Property Transactions and the New Regime

Richard Harwood Barrister, Chambers of Lionel Read QC, 1 Serjeants' Inn

Martin Edwards Barrister, Chambers of Lionel Read QC, 1 Serjeants' Inn

William Upton Barrister, Chambers of Lionel Read QC, 1 Serjeants' Inn

It is essential that property and commercial practitioners fully understand the law and practicalities of dealing with contaminated land. This substantial book puts the new Guidance in its Regulatory context, and interprets it for practitioners.

Key contents: – The new contaminated land regime: How does it work? Who is liable? What does it mean for developers, landowners, local authorities and professionals? – Water, waste and statutory nuisance – Private law rights: nuisance, negligence, *Rylands* v *Fletcher* – Planning and contaminated land – Protecting property and corporate transactions.

£42 2000 ISBN 1 85811 206 0

Tenant Default under Commercial Leases, Third Edition

Andrew E Parsons Solicitor, Partner, Radcliffes

Tenant default is an area of major concern to landlords and their professional advisers. The cross over of landlord and tenant law and the process of debt collection brings to the fore a series of practical and legal problems for the professional.

Once the tell-tale signs are there – non-payment of rent of a service charge, failure to repair, breach of user covenants or insolvency – prompt action is needed. This book was written to bring together in an easy to use and practical format the materials necessary to effect that action. Succinct and well laid-out chapters provide self-contained explanations of the options available and advice on how to proceed.

Well-drafted Precedents are provided. Changes since the second edition: the Civil Procedure Rules and their accompanying Practice Direction have affected tenant default actions. This edition has been brought thoroughly into line with the Rule and terminological changes that the Reforms have effected, as well as taking into account new law. Individuals, solicitors, surveyors, local authority officers and all others involved in the construction or management of property will find the work invaluable.

£44 2000 ISBN 1 85811 240 0

emis professional publishing, 31–33 stonehills house, welwyn garden city, al8 6pu
tel: 01707–334823 fax: 01707–335022 dx 144000 welwyn garden city
order any title online at *www.emispp.com*
contact us by email at *sales@emispp.com*

Seneca CM – revolutionary software from emis it

Seneca CM is a complete Contact, file and activity Management system for legal practice. An elegant, one-stop solution that is flexible enough to handle even the most unusual work types, Seneca CM from emis intellectual technology has been intuitively designed to work just the way you do.

Seneca CM is designed to handle any type of file in organisations of any type and size, whether private practice, in-house or local government, including unusual file types. We look at your documents and workflows, and offer a bespoke system to suit your needs.

The system provides a wide range of legal functionality within one single package, including Microsoft Word and digital dictation. Seneca CM allows you to integrate new technology into your contact management, such as multi-media files and biometric technology. Integration with Seneca Electronic Publishing (EP) provides the latest up to date legal information at your fingertips. Seneca EP is included free during the first year of installation of Seneca CM.

For more see *www.emisit.com* or contact us on 08701 225 525

www.ingramcontent.com/pod-product-compliance
Lightning Source LLC
LaVergne TN
LVHW011803200926
848484LV00003B/773